BANJO PATERSON

Banjo Paterson

His poetry and prose

Selected and introduced by

Richard Hall

ALLEN & UNWIN

First published 1993
Allen & Unwin Pty Ltd
9 Atchison Street, St Leonards, NSW 2065 Australia

National Library of Australia
Cataloguing-in-Publication entry:

Paterson, A.B. (Andrew Barton), 1864–1941.
  Banjo Paterson selection.

  Includes index.
  ISBN 1 86373 369 8.

  I. Hall, Richard, 1937– . II. Title.

A821.2

Set in 10/12.5 Century Schoolbook
by Graphicraft Typesetters, Hong Kong
Printed by SRM Production Services Sdn Bhd, Malaysia

Contents

*... the vision splendid of the sunlit plains extended
And at night the wondrous glory of the everlasting stars.*

The Sporting Life
... I'll never back horses at seven to four ...

The Reporter's Eye
... the sufferer's face grows an ashen grey. The doctor hurries off, and you are left along with the dying man ...

The Banjo *v*. Henry Lawson
So you're back from up the country, Mister Lawson . . .

The Comic Side
*. . . 'Murder! Bloody murder!' yelled the man from
    Ironbark . . .*

Last Words

Andrew Barton Paterson—His Fortunate Life

When Banjo Paterson died on February 5, 1941, he had £221/17/1 in the bank and liabilities of £46. When a block of land at Eden on the South Coast, valued at £26, and some personal effects including jewellery were taken into account, the total estate of the balladist who had sold more books than any of his contemporaries or almost all of his successors came out at £303/3/1. A lifetime of writing had brought him little in monetary terms. Paterson was a tenant who had never owned the flats and houses he had lived in. In the way in which these things happen in Australia there have always been those who liked to set an image of a rich and secure Paterson against that of a poor and destitute Henry Lawson. At its most extreme this notion finds expression in the claim that Paterson could never have written 'Waltzing Matilda' because his class background meant that he could never have been as sympathetic to the underdog, in this case a swagman who had stolen a sheep from the squatter.

Lawson is seen as the classic failure, but in a different way Paterson was also a failure, particularly if measured by the same cramped and ungenerous society of between-wars Australia, a society very different from that of the 1890s when their talents had first flowered. Lawson died in 1922, a wreck of a man, while Paterson survived until

1941. In its 1940 edition, that arbiter of status in a small
dominion, *Who's Who*, dropped Paterson from its entries.
When he died the obituarial adjective the *Sydney Morn-
ing Herald* chose was the patronising 'cheery'.

The literary page on the following Saturday didn't
mention one Australian book, reflecting reading tastes
set in London. The lead book review was of *White Cliffs*,
a verse–narrative romance about an American woman
who had married an Englishman 'of good but undistin-
guished family', and the war. The two latest poetry col-
lections of Sigfried Sassoon and Herbert Read were
reviewed. Literature was represented by a worthy book
titled *Augustans and Romantics 1689–1939*.

There is probably something in the idea of national traits;
it could be argued that some of Andrew Barton Paterson's
reserve derived from his lowland Scots forebears. The
family came from generations of farmers in the stony
ground of Lanarkshire, although one of its members,
William Paterson, stepped outside to become a banker,
one of the founders of the Bank of England. He also tried
his hand at colonisation, raising finance for a Scottish
colony established at Darien on the Isthmus of Panama
in 1698—ignoring the inconvenience of Spanish owner-
ship. Hundreds died from pestilence and Spanish pun-
itive action. The investors of Scotland, large and small,
lost some £250 000. There was a family tradition, re-
counted by Banjo Paterson, that the investors so admired
William Paterson, even though they had lost all, that
they subscribed £10 000 to help him reestablish himself.
It is a good family story and like many just that—a story.
A historian of the affair, John Preeble, records that
Paterson and those few who returned with him to Ed-
inburgh were met with 'abuse and disgust' and that
Paterson himself had to flee to London, where he eked
out a living as a maths teacher in Soho. Later he acted
as an agent and advocate for the successful English

campaign to abolish the separate Scots parliament, and was rewarded by the government with a grant of thousands of pounds.

Whatever William Paterson did with his money, by the beginning of the nineteenth century Banjo's grandfather was a soldier and then an officer with the East India Company. The poet's father, Andrew Bogle Paterson, was born in Scotland in 1833 and came to Australia about 1850, together with his brother John, a half-sister and two half-brothers from their father's first marriage. They evidently did not have enough capital to take up land in the way of those better-off settlers coming to the colony who were creating the squatting class. It was 1860 before Andrew Bogle and John took up two adjacent runs, Buckenbah (or Buckinbah) and Curra Creek at Yeoval in the central west of New South Wales. After a decade in the colony Andrew had acquired his stake though at 4d an acre rent per year it was hardly prime land. Still, great squatting fortunes had been built on less promising beginnings. Within two years Andrew married Rose Barton from Boree Nyrang station about forty miles to the south. Although not particularly well run by her father, Boree Nyrang was a well established property with a comfortable homestead. The family's connections were good and Rose's father, Robert Barton, had brought £20 000 in capital to Australia.

The home Rose Paterson came to on the flat dusty plains at Buckenbah was anything but substantial. The ruins of the house still stand because the brothers built it with local granite in the dry-stone style of their native Scotland. The home was small, no bigger than the dining room in a wealthy squatter's house. Andrew Barton Paterson was born two years later, in 1864, in Rose's aunt's house at Narambla, near Orange, forty miles away. Her aunt had married a miller who had built a large redbrick windmill on a hill overlooking a pleasant river, with a house a lot bigger than Buckenbah.

When the young mother returned life was made harder by the frequent absences of her husband who, striving to succeed, had taken an interest with John and another brother in a property hundreds of miles away in Queensland. It was not only Lawson's selectors' wives who were left alone. While Buckenbah was stone compared to the selectors' usual wattle and daub, it was about the same size. There were shepherds in their huts in the outpaddocks, but it was still very different from the well-staffed Boree Nyrang, where Rose had grown up. By now her father had died and her mother had moved to Sydney.

Later Banjo Paterson made it clear that he didn't remember Buckenbah with any joy, unlike Illalong, his next home. Some time about the beginning of 1869, Andrew Bogle Paterson had decided to break his partnership with his brother, raised a bank loan and took a property at Illalong Creek, near Yass on the main Wagga road. In all Paterson's memories, Illalong remained the magic place of childhood.

But while for Barty, as he was known in the family, and his brother and sisters when they came, Illalong was a place of happiness, for his father it saw the end of his hopes of riches and independence. By the end of that year the bank had foreclosed. Illalong was sold to the owner of two larger adjacent stations. The new owner merged the three properties and made Andrew Bogle Paterson the manager. He was to live there for the rest of his life. There were different gradations among station managers: some were mere overseers, some were men of substance in the community. Andrew Bogle Paterson seems to have been more the latter. He made a reputation as a sheep breeder and was a member of the Union Club in Sydney, distinctly a gentleman's club. But for all that, he was the employee of an absentee landlord. Managers didn't pile up riches, they didn't go Home regularly with their families as did the Anglo-Australian squattocracy, and they didn't leave big legacies to their children. One story Paterson was to tell made it clear that expenditure was closely watched in the household. His father brought home the complete works of Sir Walter Scott and Charles Dickens. When Rose expressed concern at the cost, Paterson senior responded that he had bought the children an education.

The homestead, Illalong Creek, survived until the late twenties. Photographs show it as larger than Buckenbah, but still nothing like the scale of a von Guerard property. It was of red box gum slab-timber construction. Some of the planks, used now as fencing around the new home, show the remnants of fading wallpaper and white wash. A huge gnarled wisteria survives from those days, forming a spacious canopy, and nearer the creek are a couple of white cedars. Buckenbah also has several white cedars which have contrived to survive alongside the ruins of that house. The tree must have meant something in the family, because Andrew Bogle's tombstone in the cemetery at Binalong, a few miles from Illalong, bears a representation of a white cedar sprig.

When he went to Illalong Paterson still had no brothers or sisters. His first school was at Binalong, the nearest town. His classmates were mostly from the poorer selector families, many of them Irish Catholic in that area. Pedagogic method in the one-teacher school relied on brute force. One stroke of the cane came for not being able to answer a question, two for lateness and three for telling lies. In 1872, at the age of eight, Barty was taken to the races, a day that he remembered for the rest of his life, even to the taste of the ginger-beer. Paterson was henceforth a racing man and although it is heretical to say it, he probably loved the racing world more than he loved his ballads.

His grandmother, Emily Barton, after the death of her husband had established herself in Sydney at a cottage in Gladesville, then a semi-rural suburb on the Parramatta River. Barty needed an education of wider scope than the three Rs of the country school but a boarding school would cost more than a set of Dickens or Scott. The solution was for him to stay with his grand-mother. After a brief and it seems unhappy time at a prep school, Barty started in 1874 at Sydney Grammar School, a day-school in the city. Grammar was a private school and like most of its type took its inspiration from the public schools of England, but it was unusual among such schools in being a day-school in the heart of a city. The boys found their way through the teeming streets of what was already a big city: it was a long way from Buckenbah and Illalong. Most of the boys were sons of professionals or the better-off merchant class and them-selves the professionals and businessmen of the future.

Emily Barton was financially independent and well connected. The social set of Sydney, still relatively small, came to her garden parties, its children to her charades. While young Barty could not hope for a big inheritance he was growing up with a secure place in what passed for the establishment. Emily Barton herself read widely, wrote some poetry and maintained a good library.

In the country the boy had inevitably grown up on a horse and Gladesville was still country enough for him to be always on horseback. Half a mile or so up the hill was Gladesville Hospital for the insane. Edward Betts, the deputy superintendent, was one of the best amateur horsemen in the colony as well as a treasurer of the Sydney Turf Club, over the river at Rosehill, and a com-mittee member of the Australian Jockey Club and the Sydney Hunt Club. Betts was a friend of the family and Barty became his protegé. For his time, Betts was an enlightened doctor. He tried to open up the hospital, running dances for patients which were attended by young outsiders like Barty.

Paterson wasn't a prefect at Sydney Grammar—per-haps he was too easygoing. At the end of his time he sat for a university entrance examination but failed in his hopes of obtaining a bursary, which would have paid his fees. He failed in English grammar, but got a 'higher pass' in English. He could have worked as a jackaroo, with the prospect of a manager's job—the days when runs were out there for the taking by would-be squatters had long since gone—but Paterson was to make it clear over the years that he had a pretty cynical view of the jackaroo's status, and for that matter of working for an absentee landlord. In the absence of a bursary, the only path into a prosperous profession was to be articled to a solicitor, and in 1880 Paterson did just that. His career seemed set—in Australia a solicitor with the right connections could hope not only for status but also for an affluent old age.

Barty had gone back to Illalong over the years for his holidays. While he was away in Sydney a brother had been born, and four sisters. His mother had brothers with properties further out where he also holidayed, so the young boy saw a lot of New South Wales.

Apart from the amenities of the social life, Sydney in the 1880s was a highly politicised city, which played its politics with a passion and vehemence that can make today's disputes seem polite. The press reflected this climate. The *Bulletin*, a weekly journal founded in 1880, quickly established itself as a trenchant participant in the political struggle. Its literary role was slower to develop. In particular the *Bulletin* spoke with an unabashedly Australian nationalist voice, quick to mock those who tugged the forelock to the Old Country.

Early in February 1885 the news reached Sydney of the death of General Gordon in Khartoum. Amidst great patriotic fervour a force of 750 was raised and dispatched to the Sudan in two weeks to fight alongside the avenging English. Not everyone was enthused. The *Bulletin* certainly was not, nor was the young Paterson, who supplied the magazine with four stanzas complaining that

Australia was 'in arms against the freeman's right' and that the contingent was striking 'a blow for tyranny and wrong'. There was a fierce reference to 'England's degenerate generals'. For this, his first contribution published, the young articled clerk wisely chose a pseudonym: articles have been cancelled for much less. The poem was called 'El Mahdi to the Australian Troops', so Paterson logically enough signed it El Mahdi, the *nom de geurre* of the Islamic religious leader who was inspiring the Sudanese. Anthologists have avoided this poem, which is rather a pity because even though it is pretty terrible verse, it is a nice piece of angry young man's writing.

Maybe he owned up at the Sydney Hunt Club, maybe he didn't, but in his next published attempt in June 1886 Paterson was again on the radical side with another political poem, 'The Bushfire—An Allegory', a commentary on the English government's law and order coercion policy in Ireland. The allegory is a bit murky—a squatter is running around putting out a lot of bushfires and a wise bystander tells him to go to the source of the fires rather than just put them out. The verses are memorable only for the fact that the articled clerk chose 'The Banjo' as a pseudonym—again, young solicitors were not supposed to be on the side of Irish Home Rule. As he explained it later, the name had nothing to with the musical instrument, but came from the name of a horse at Illalong that allegedly had a past racing career.

'The Banjo' returned with 'A Dream of the Melbourne Cup' in October of that year. It is the first really confident ballad in the Paterson style, sardonic with a good come-all-ye opening: 'Bring me a quart of colonial beer'. At the same time he submitted a satire on pastoral true love, 'The Mylora Elopement'. He was summoned to the office of Jules François Archibald, probably the best editor Australia has ever had, a man with an uncanny capacity to pick talent and more importantly the persistence to make it grow, by coaxing, cajoling and cutting.

As Paterson told the story more than fifty years later:

> Did I know anything about the bush? I told him I
> had been reared there. 'All right,' he said. 'Have
> a go at the bush. Have a go at anything that
> strikes you. Don't write anything like other people
> if you can help it. Let's see what you can do.'

Paterson was aboard what was already a national insti-
tution. In March the next year he tried an indifferent
political satire and in April he came out with 'Only a
Jockey'. His sharp eye had picked up a report from
Melbourne: 'Richard Benson, a jockey, aged fourteen,
while riding William Tell in his training was thrown and
killed. The horse is luckily uninjured.' The poem opened
tightly but became a little florid at the end, invoking
God. Paterson, a rider in days before helmets, was later
to return to the theme of death and injury on the track.
In 1894 he wrote a ballad elegy for the death of Tommy
Corrigan, by contrast with the fourteen-year-old the best
known jockey in Australia, who died in a steeplechase in
Melbourne. As a sporting journalist he wrote again of
how jockeys risked their lives for pitiful returns.

There was a long break until Christmas 1888, when
'The Banjo' came back with 'Old Pardon, the Son of
Reprieve', a happier tale of an old racehorse in retirement.
This was the first of his ballads to enter the reciters'
repertoires. Before radio and television, the nineteenth
century, making much of its own fun, was crazy about
recitals, with a plethora of collections designed to help
the (usually male) reciters shine. The ballads could range
from the stirringly historical through the sentimental to
the humorous.

If 'Old Pardon' became a favourite, 'Clancy of the
Overflow', published a few months later, became central
to the repertoire, only surpassed in popularity by 'The
Man from Snowy River'. Clancy introduced a recurring
theme in Paterson's verse: the narrator is in a city office

(suspiciously like a solicitor's office as there seems to be no hard taskmaster superior) pining for the bush, a place of freedom and beauty. Clancy, the bushman, his friend of years gone by—still out there—is blessed:

> *. . . he sees the vision splendid of the sunlit plains*
> *   extended*
> *And at night the wondrous glory of the everlasting*
> *   stars . . .*

While his friend in the office is exposed to:

> *. . . the foetid air and gritty of the dusty, dirty city*
> *Through the open window floating, spreads its foulness*
> *   over all.*

This version of the Australian pastoral idyll, plenty have pointed out, is perhaps a bit too glowing, but then that is the nature of the ballad.

Throughout the rest of that year the *Bulletin* published half a dozen of Paterson's humorous verses, but in prose the young solicitor published under his own name a piece of savage polemic, a criticism of colonial society, especially the system of landholding and the place of absentee landlords. In *Australia for the Australians. A Political Pamphlet, Showing the necessity for Land Reform combined with Protection*, the man who paid for the printing did not hide behind a pseudonym, but identified himself on the title page as A.B. Paterson, Solicitor, Sydney. The present system of land tenure was a 'rotten, absurd system', which locked up the land to the absentees 'and left the present generation to wilderness'. The people had been driven to the cities to live in squalor. He suggested his readers should:

> . . . take a night walk round the poorer quarters of
> our large colonial cities and they will see such as
> they will never forget. They will see vice and sin
> and misery in full development. They will see
> poor people herding in wretched little shanties,

the tiny stuffy rooms fairly reeking like ovens
with the heat of our tropical summer.

The young gentleman rider told how he had planned
to 'live for a space' in one of the lower-looking boarding
houses but had only lasted one night, though women and
children had to live in similar filth and discomfort from
one year's end to another. 'Land reform and protection
should go together.' Unlike most of the squatters the
young Paterson was against lower wages and it followed
that the local manufacturers should not have to compete
with starvation wages overseas. He ended on an optimis-
tic note, affirming that 'life need not be such a very root-
hog-or-die proceeding as it now is'.

The pamphlet, out of character with the controlled,
reserved style of the rest of his life, carries no dedication,
but in June that year Paterson had suffered a tragedy
which must have focused his rage against the land system.
His father, Andrew Bogle Paterson, had stayed on at
Illalong, still the manager twenty years after he had lost
his independence and still relatively young. At 56 he
could have expected to see the new century in, but on 7
June he took an overdose of opium and died. After an
inquest the coroner, Mr Chisholm, found that Andrew
Bogle Paterson had died at Illalong of 'an overdose of
opium accidentally self-administered'.

Opium was present in both patent and prescribed
medicines of the time. One mixture alleviated diarrhoea
and another suppressed persistent chest coughs. Any
establishment like a station would have carried stocks
of these medicines. However, on forensic advice given
to me, it would be very difficult to accidentally self-
administer a fatal overdose. According to the formulas
laid down by the *British Pharmacopeia* the victim would
need to have quickly swallowed more than ten times the
normal dose, if not more.

Magistrates acting as coroners not uncommonly tried

to evade the responsibility of unequivocally finding suicide, seeking to shield the family. Mr Chisholm, in that confined country world, would have known Paterson senior and his family. Now we see suicide not as a moral failure, but as a product of a depressive illness. It was otherwise in the nineteenth century—suicide was a shame to the family. Whatever the coroner's verdict, the locals, and probably the members of the Union Club in Sydney, must have whispered speculations. So, when that year the young man railed against the 'rotten and absurd system' that had left his father another man's servant, he was mourning a death. The tragedy also provides the key to 'On Kiley's Run', which he published the following year, a poem usually seen as an uncomplicated example of the sentimental pastoral genre.

Kiley's run is the dream of the golden life: 'The swagman never turned away ... the station-hands were friends ... the boss was kindness through and through'. But then the drought and losses came and the bank foreclosed: 'Old Kiley died of a broken heart'.

There is a bitter gibe:

> *The owner lives in England now ...*
> *He knows a race-horse from a cow*
> *But that is all he knows of stock ...*
> *... he sends from town to keep*
> *the shearers' wages down ...*

Then there is the usurpation:

> *The homestead we held so dear*
> *Contains a half-paid overseer*
> *On Kiley's Run.*

Young Banjo was also prepared to have a go at religion. In later life he showed no signs of religious practice, except to marry in church. Thomas Carlyle, the prose writer Paterson admired most, was also no lover of organised religion. In the Christmas issue of the *Bulletin* in

1889 Paterson turned his satire on the Judeo–Christian ethic in a long turgid poem, 'The Scapegoat', about an Old Testament sacrificial goat that got away. It's not worth reprinting, but it would have been deeply offensive to any conservative Victorian Christian. This suited the *Bulletin*, which loved to tweak the clergy's nose.

In 1890 Paterson appeared (still under a pseudonym) between covers for the first time as a poet in *The Golden Shanty*, an anthology of *Bulletin* contributors, including Henry Lawson amongst others. In the journal itself he published eight poems and a comic story. 'The Man from Snowy River', that epic of the mountain horseman of the Monaro, came in April. There is a recurring story that Paterson grew up in the Monaro, but in fact much of his growing up was done in Sydney and Illalong itself—a long way from the Monaro.

Paterson was by now in partnership with John Street, whose establishment connections would ensure ultimate, not rapid, success. They had a wide commercial practice, including banks and shipping companies. His partner's and his own social contacts meant that the firm was destined for prosperity. Even though Sydney was then suffering from depression, sooner or later depressions end.

Meanwhile Paterson, huntsman and amateur jockey, was developing another skill—polo playing. The sport had been introduced to Melbourne in the 1870s by army officers from India, but had been slow to gain popularity. In theory it was a rich man's sport, because of the need for a stable of ponies, but some of the country teams were pretty rough and ready. Paterson's classic, 'The Geebung Polo Club', seems to have been inspired by the defeat of a team from the wealthy Western Districts of Victoria by a scruffy outback New South Wales team called the Tamarangs. In an article on polo he wrote a few years later, Paterson put himself on the side of the rough men: 'Those who have the money to purchase first-class horses cannot ride them and those who can ride them haven't got the money'.

Paterson, the first-class horseman with connections and looks, had a hectic social life. Writing in the 1950s, John Manifold, a poet and folk historian and himself a member of an old pastoral family (that team from the Western Districts beaten by the equivalent of the Geebung Polo Club had several Manifolds in it), said: 'If my grand-mother was not pulling my leg when she told me ... Paterson was highly attractive to women, and seldom out of girl trouble until he married'.

The young man had also clearly more than a passing acquaintance with pub bars and clubs. In his first book, *The Man from Snowy River*, just on one-third of the poems have some reference to drink, drinkers or bars. But for all that Paterson didn't join the Bohemian Push of *Bulletin* writers, with their clubs and drinking rituals. The bookseller James Tyrrell, who knew everyone, wrote years later: 'Old Rod Quinn [a poet] who was the Bo-hemian of the Bohemians, used to say to me: "Banjo was never with us", or "Banjo never came along", or "Banjo was never one of us"'. Everything we know of Paterson's life shows him as convivial but controlled, unlike the man with whom his name is often coupled—Henry Lawson.

Lawson, it is not unfair to say, was not a man who could hold his drink, although in the happy, boozy world of the young men of literary Sydney in those early days that was not particularly noticeable. In 1892, as Paterson told it later, Lawson suggested they could make a bit of money in contributor's payments from the *Bulletin* by setting up a duel, with Paterson on the side of the Bush à la Clancy, and with Lawson writing from the sour per-spective of the battling selectors. Conceived as a joke, by the end, at least on Lawson's side, there was more than a tinge of bitterness. Paterson held out the olive branch, suggesting that they might give it all up and 'vermilionize the bars'. Other bards bought into the debate before J.F. Archibald closed the whole thing down.

That Christmas The Banjo turned to lighter things, producing 'The Man from Ironbark', a parable of the innocent boy from the Bush in the Big City, probably the most popular of his humorous pieces. On the social turmoil of the strikes of 1891 and 1892 the young solicitor was silent, but in June 1893 he dashed off a sharp piece of sarcasm on the bank collapses: 'Reconstruction from a Farmer's Point of View'. The rest of year there was only light verse, as with 'When Dacey Rode the Mule'. In 1894 Paterson's production petered out, but early in 1895 Archibald, always keen to help his flock, sent Paterson along with a letter to George Robertson, partner in the bookstore Angus and Robertson.

George Robertson has had an extraordinarily good press in the history of Australian literature, probably because in his later years he was assiduous in promoting the image of himself a visionary lover of Australian literature, much put upon by various writers. The truth is that far from seeking out his two most prolific and profitable writers, Banjo Paterson and Henry Lawson, it was they who sought him out. Robertson was so cautious and unvisionary in dealing with Paterson that he did not offer a royalty arrangement, that is, a percentage of sales, but merely a half share of the profits after all expenses had been met. Paterson took the deal. It became known that Paterson was going to publish, and one of the Bohemians, Le Gay Brereton, sent Lawson a letter reporting that Robertson had made Paterson a good offer and that Lawson should follow his initiative. Having done his sums and assessed his man, Robertson offered an outright up-front payment for copyright, to which Lawson at first agreed. On learning of Paterson's share deal, however, he demanded the same and got it for his first book of poetry and the next of prose. Robertson rebuked Paterson for letting the terms of their private deal become known.

Not long after his approach to Robertson, The Banjo ventured for the first time into reporting, his other vocation, which was to support him for most of his life. It was an account of an illegal dog-fight out in the Botany Bay sandhills just after dawn. A couple of hundred Sydney sportsmen attended, ready to run if the police appeared. The piece is almost a model bit of reporting, an account of a bloody clash between two bull terriers. Archibald, however, did not succeed in getting any more such low-life contributions. In a few months The Banjo's disguise was to be penetrated and perhaps it was not possible to have a respectable solicitor attending illegal events—so posterity missed Paterson on two-up.

Waiting for publication of *The Man from Snowy River*, Paterson made a trip through western Queensland, partly business and partly pleasure: he had a fiancée at Winton, Sarah Riley. With a group they travelled to Dagworth Station, where Paterson for the first time heard the slang phrase 'waltzing Matilda', which described the wandering bush worker carrying his few possessions in a roll of blankets called his swag—hence the term swagman. Swagmen were not overly scrupulous about the squatters' property rights in their sheep, when sheep were the only meal around. Local folklore included the story of a wanted man who drowned himself in a billabong rather than be taken by the police. Music, songs and charades were part of station entertainment and one night Paterson improvised 'Waltzing Matilda', with some others dressing the parts. One of Paterson's biographers, Clement Semmler, effectively puts the case for Paterson's authorship of 'Waltzing Matilda', refuting other claims. There has been almost as much controversy about the derivation of the tune as about the death of Mozart. At the time Paterson thought of the song as nothing more than a bit of fun. He didn't bother to put it into *The Man from Snowy River*.

This first book came out in October to sudden and

deafening acclaim. The initial 1250 copies went immediately and Robertson paid the author £35 for his share of the profits and printed another thousand.

The *Bulletin*'s A.G. Stephens contrasted The Banjo with the Cavalier lyricists and even Melbourne newspapers praised the New South Wales balladist. Back Home, *The Times* gave its imprimatur by comparing Paterson with Kipling. Although Kipling has commonly been cited as an influence on Paterson, the fact is that Paterson was older than Kipling and publishing ballads before Kipling achieved fame. Rather we should look back to the Border Ballads and Sir Walter Scott for influence, or even further to traditional ballads like 'Sir Patrick Spens', which Paterson later used as a framework for a joke poem about Santa Claus.

In prose Paterson professed to have been most impressed by the work of the nineteenth century historian Thomas Carlyle, taking not only his anti-clericalism but also something of his obsession with men of destiny like Cromwell. Among the poets of the century his favourites were Tennyson and Longfellow; somewhat surprisingly, he also liked the florid Algernon Swinburne.

In January 1896, just after he came to his first fame, Paterson gave a revealing interview to Bernard Espinasse, from the Melbourne magazine *Table Talk*, who admitted catching his subject by surprise in the office. Perhaps because it was all new, Paterson gave the most frankest interview of his life. He talked of reading Darwin's *Origin of Species* with enthusiasm; of reading books from the eighteenth century, especially Laurence Sterne's *Sentimental Journey*. Sitting in the office he was reading *Degeneration* by Max Nordau, open at page 252. Nordau was one of the flock of pseudo-scientific social Darwinists popular at the turn of the century, whose theories formed the basis of modern racism. Paterson, while never rabid on the subject, was impressed, as were many of his contemporaries, by these racial theories dressed up as science. It shows in some of his travel writings. An extract from that page 252 which Paterson was reading when Espinasse surprised him gives the flavour: 'The sexual instinct which forces an individual to seek for another individual is as little altruism as the hunger which incites the hunter to follow an animal and eat it.'

The most revealing comment from this interview came when Paterson was asked why he had left the country:

> I soon saw that there wasn't a livelihood to be
> gained on the land. Everyone who goes in for
> farming right out comes to grief sooner or later.
> At best it is only a continual struggle. My idea
> always was to have enough to live on comfortably,
> that if I wanted a thing which didn't cost too
> much I could get it. And station life didn't seem
> to promise that way at all. So while I was in the
> thick of the bush I didn't let it get such a hold on
> me that I couldn't leave it.

It was the pessimist of Kiley's Run speaking rather than the optimist of Clancy. Espinasse wasn't to know it but Paterson was talking about his father as much as about himself.

At the end of this interview for *Table Talk* The Banjo showed that all the praise had not gone to his head when he came out with a blunt: 'I am not a poet. I am a versifier.'

After the excitement of publication and success Paterson was not stirred to great energy for some time. In the next two years he published five poems and two stories in the *Bulletin. The Man from Snowy River* continued to walk out of the shops all over Australia as well as in Britain. By July 1897 13 000 copies had been sold. Still the financial returns were far from what he would have received as income from his legal partnership, with its good connections: in 1897 he received but £98 from his book's sales. One result of his popularity had been a flow of correspondence, accompanied by gifts such as possum and emu skins with which he carpeted his office. As well, there was 'the plume of a white crane', which he displayed.

The flow of correspondence included not only the writers' own attempts at doggerel but also a number of old bush songs, which stimulated Paterson to put a proposal to Robertson for Paterson himself to collect a selection. The famed generous guardian of Australia's cultural heritage bestirred himself to offer his best-selling author a £20 advance and one-third of the profits. For that inducement Paterson didn't exactly hurry—it was 1905 before the collection came out.

Although Paterson was not involved socially with the literary Bohemians, he was very much involved in one of their ventures, the *Antipodean*, a monthly magazine. He edited the Christmas issue for 1897, collecting contributions from Henry Lawson, Edward Dyson, Rod Quinn and Steele Rudd. The same issue carried an enlightened and sympathetic article on 'The Customs of the Australian Aborigine'.

An earlier issue that year of the *Antipodean* contained a comic verse under his old pen-name of The Banjo, which has been overlooked by anthologists, perhaps because of its crass commercialism. The verse, suitably illustrated, sent up the cycling craze. 'The Scorcher [as in fast rider] and the Howling Swell' began:

> *The Scorcher and the Howling Swell were*
> *   riding through the land:*
> *They wept like any thing to see the hills*
> *   on every hand.*
> *'If these were only levelled down,' they*
> *   said, 'it would be grand.'*

They met up with some ladies, whom the Scorcher tried to impress by riding fast up the hills. The ladies strove to keep up and then complained:

> 'It's very rude,' the ladies said, 'To ride
>   as fast as that.'
> 'For all of us are out of breath and some
>   of us are fat.'
> 'Cheer-up, my ladies gay,' the Howling
>   Swell replied.
> 'Behold a tea-shop by the way with
>   Globe Brand Tea inside.
> 'And all who drink Globe Brand Tea up
>   any hill can ride.'
> And every lady in the band revived on
>   Globe Brand Tea.
> That Adderly and Dawson sell in George
>   Street, near the Quay.
> And Howling Swells and Scorchers
>   both proclaim its purity.

Well, it was one way to get advertisements for a literary magazine. His selection of a story by Steele Rudd on the other hand, before Rudd had gained fame from *On Our Selection*, shows editorial prescience.

In 1898 Paterson strayed furthest yet from home, to the Northern Territory, on a journalism commission from a steamship company to write a sportsman's guide to the Territory's pleasures, such as buffalo-shooting. Apart from the commissioned material he sent back a number of other articles, and stored up material that he was to recycle decades later. Then it was back to the dingy little office in Bond Street, where apart from the old bush songs he was working on a novel and another collection of verse.

The Transvaal War, as it was called at first, gave him the chance to escape the law again, this time for good. Paterson negotiated an advance of £150 from his publisher, on account of his three outstanding projects, and arranged to sail as a war correspondent for the *Sydney Morning Herald* and the *Argus* in Melbourne.

One of the chores of Paterson's last months in the law was a doomed attempt to instil some fairness into Angus and Robertson's treatment of Henry Lawson. While Lawson's *In the Days When the World was Wide* had not sold as well as *The Man from Snowy River*, he also had a successful prose collection in *While the Billy Boils*. Lawson subsequently sold not only his copyright for the first two books but also the copyright to short stories and verse, as they were written, usually for £5. It was a good deal for Robertson—Lawson, like Paterson, was to be reprinted again and again. An analysis of just how Lawson was manipulated and exploited is beyond the scope of this introduction, but it can be said that a reading of the financial records within the Angus and Robertson holdings in the Mitchell Library shows that if Lawson had been receiving royalties on the same scale as Paterson, he would have received thousands of pounds more in income.

In 1899 Paterson, as solicitor acting for Lawson, wrote to Robertson seeking renegotiation to allow at least some proportion of royalties to Lawson. Robertson rejected the idea and seems to have cast aspersions on Lawson's quality. The usually easy-going Paterson was terse in his reply: 'I think that you are too critical as to the quality of his last pieces, what I read were distinctly good: you were very keen on getting his work and now that you have got it at your own price you don't like it.'

But Lawson was to lose his advocate, because Paterson no longer wanted to be anyone's advocate. Even before the Transvaal War had started the Australian colonies had agreed that they would send a joint contingent of 2500 soldiers, and they were ready in October. Paterson went with them, taking three horses. He never returned to Bond Street. The man who fifteen years before had railed against the degenerate British generals was going to war.

In his own idiosyncratic way Paterson proved to be a rather unusual war correspondent. He saw the war with a cold eye and was far from being merely a patriotic booster. Expensive cables provided the press of the day with the highlights. Dispatches from correspondents like Paterson came by sea mail and could be more discursive.

One of his first reports gave a long treatment of the Boer case against the British. He spoke with Olive Schreiner, whose book *The Story of an African Farm* was something of a classic, well known outside Africa. He quoted the Afrikaans author extensively, without any censorship or toning down. Among other things Schreiner said, 'This is a capitalist war. They want to gain control of the Rand and the mines . . . It is a monstrous war . . . I cannot understand at all why you came here light-heartedly to shoot down other colonists of whom you know nothing.'

Paterson also met Kipling in Africa. Although he always expressed respect for Kipling and cultivated his acquaintance later for Kipling could be very useful in England, at their first meeting in South Africa Paterson cast a rather cold eye on Kipling. He spoke of the poet laying 'aside the pen of the author for the carpet-bag of the politician', and contrived to send up Kipling's call for Australians to flock to South Africa so that after the war the Boers could be outnumbered. A bloodthirsty Kipling explained that the Tommies didn't want the war to end quickly because they wanted revenge, their 'money back'. Later, back with the Australians, Paterson mused that they, unlike Kipling's Tommies, were not panting for a wider war. More than three decades later, when Angus and Robertson republished some of the Boer War material, somehow Paterson's critical perspective on Kipling had disappeared, censored out.

In other material Paterson criticised the medical arrangements and noted how in battle the wounded officer got more attention than the Tommy. He also noted the thick-headedness of British military intelligence officers. He wrote of the mis-handling of the Boers who had surrendered, criticism which he had no hesitation in

repeating on his return to Australia in September 1900
in interviews and a series of lectures around Australia.

In April 1901 there was a report that Paterson was con-
sidering standing as a Protectionist for the country seat
of Braidwood, but nothing more came of it. It must have
been one of the expedients he considered to avoid return-
ing to the law. The end of his lecture tour forced him to
what was his final choice—writing. He made the decision
by accepting a commission from the *Sydney Morning
Herald* for a series of articles on the New South Wales
countryside, mainly boosting irrigation. There were also
the three projects outstanding for Angus and Robertson.

Then in July his departure for China was announced.
Australia had sent a naval contingent to join the allies
in the Boxer War the previous year, but it had arrived
after the raising of the siege of Peking (now Beijing) and
had returned to Australia in April. However, the treaty
talks had dragged on and there were rumours of war.
It was announced that Mr Paterson would cover any
war, but if peace prevailed he would go to Europe via
the Trans-Siberian railway.

In Peking Paterson met George 'Chinese' Morrison,
certainly the most famous Australian journalist of the
time and one of the few people of whom it could be said
the laconic Paterson came close to hero-worshipping.
Morrison was more than just a journalist—he was a man
of action, who had walked across Australia, been speared
in New Guinea, and worked around the world as a ship's
doctor before finishing up as *The Times*' correspondent in
Peking. A vigorous imperialist, with a rigid sense of the
superiority of the Anglo-Saxon, Morrison's dispatches
influenced policy in London, while in Peking he ma-
nipulated diplomats and Chinese officials almost at will.

War did not eventuate, and Paterson went to London
by sea in November, the worsening weather in Siberia
making the Trans-Siberian trip untenable. At the end of

the month an enthusiastic Paterson wrote to Robertson announcing his appointment as Australian correspondent for *The Times*: 'that is if it doesn't fall through'. He was right to be cautious; the appointment never came. It would have been not just a matter of prestige—such a retainer would have provided a secure income. The only mention of Paterson that can be found in *The Times'* archives today is a note of two payments, each of £25, in September and October 1902. When an appointment was made, at a retainer of £100 a month, in January 1904, it went to Arthur José, who edited for Angus and Robertson. This could hardly have pleased Paterson— apart from anything else José had been critical of the manuscript of a still unpublished novel, criticism which had provoked Paterson to ask that José should not handle it because of his lack of a sense of humour. José certainly shows up as a pompous man: a few years later he published *A History of Australasia*, probably the worst and dullest ever published—a not inconsiderable feat.

In 1902 Paterson raised some more money from interstate lectures, as well as more from journalism. Towards the end of the year his second book of verse, *Rio Grande's Last Race and other Verses*, was published. It was praised and sold well enough—The Banjo was an institution—but still the enthusiasm was not quite as great as for *The Man from Snowy River*.

Saltbush Bill returned; it contained some Boer War poems, the best being 'With French to Kimberley', as well as a swag of humorous verses, including 'Mulga Bill's Bicycle', which came to rival 'The Man from Ironbark' in popularity.

There was in this volume one poem, 'He Giveth his Beloved Sleep', which stands apart from Paterson's other verse in its religious tone. A meditation on the biblical text of the title, it is a gentle, soft poem, without any irony, ending:

For, at the last, beseeching Christ to save us,
We turn with deep
Heartfelt thanksgiving unto God, who gave us
The Gift of Sleep.

It was, although there is no clue in the book, a last
farewell to Andrew Bogle Paterson. That text is inscribed
on his tombstone at Binalong along with the white cedar
sprig.

Rio Grande's Last Race quickly covered the advance
Paterson had got before going to the Transvaal. But in
January 1903 his money problems were settled when he
was appointed editor of the *Evening News*. His position
and status were now as secure as if he had stayed in the
law. The *News* was Sydney's first evening newspaper,
having been founded in 1867. It was usually liberal pro-
tectionist in politics, and livelier in tone than, say, the
Sydney Morning Herald, carrying court cases and police
news. Paterson made a few innovations, bringing in Lionel
Lindsay as an illustrator and increasing the turf news.
Lionel's brother Norman, who got to know Paterson about
this time, describes him:

> A tall man with a finely built, muscular body,
> moving with the ease of perfectly co-ordinated
> reflexes. Black hair, dark eyes, a long finely
> articulated nose, an ironic mouth, a dark
> pigmentation of the skin due to the prime
> affliction of his life—bile. Every morning he
> suffered its effect of nausea until he had got rid of
> its accumulation.

A colleague on the paper, Claude Mackay, writing years
later, gave a different perspective from Lindsay. Paterson
sat in his office at a jumbled, untidy desk, where 'he
hated being left by himself ... anyone who came in for a
yarn [was] greeted like a long-lost brother'.

With his income assured, Paterson could marry and
did so in April. His bride was Alice Walker, a grazier's
daughter from Tenterfield, whom he had met on his

lecture tour. She was reputed to be as good a rider as Paterson himself. The engagement to Sarah Riley, she of the 'Waltzing Matilda' trip, had ended after seven years—maybe she tired of waiting for Paterson to finish his travels.

Apart from his salary Paterson was getting some royalties now from *Rio Grande's Last Race*—£75 on the eve of his marriage. In 1905 *The Old Bush Songs* was published and promptly sold 5000 copies. There was enough money to live on and pay the rent of a large two-storey house with tennis court in Woollahra (Paterson was a keen tennis player), though there were still recurrent requests to Robertson for advances on royalties.

But there was a difficulty with this new life: Paterson's name had been made with his poetry and thoughtful, discursive pieces of reporting. He had sent back letters from South Africa, not cables. Being an editor of an evening newspaper required different skills. Claude Mackay wrote of Paterson, 'anyone less attuned to evening journalism would have been hard to find'. So in 1906 Paterson was pushed sideways to edit the associated *Town and Country Journal*. The journal boasted a circulation three times that of any other weekly newspaper in Australia and was directed at a rural audience. At 6d for 60 pages it was good value if you liked a deadly dull newspaper, with paragraphs like: 'William Byrnes, aged 63, employed at the Riverstone Meat Works, dropped dead at his residence at Riverstone.' There were hundreds of paragraphs like that under the heading of 'Round the Country', as well as a column on 'Bush Fires'. It was a scissors-and-paste reprint paper. Editorship would not have been onerous. The only literary elements were reprints of hack commercial short stories. Humour came from the advertisements: 'Ageing with piles—a drover praises Zam-Buck'.

Paterson was intelligent enough to know that he had been sidelined, even humiliated. It was not a job that

Morrison of *The Times* would have taken. In 1908 Paterson decided to get out, forgetting his 1896 pessimism about prospects in the bush. In June 1908 he wrote to Robertson: 'I am going in for a sheep station and want to raise as much cash as I can. Will you make me an offer for my copyright in *Snowy River* and other books with you . . . I have about £100 in books and pictures I might also put in; won't want them up there.' (In 1896 he had told the *Table Talk* reporter that he planned to build up a collection of pictures.)

In 1939 in his reminiscences Paterson wrote of a kind of nervous breakdown at that time. His biographer Clement Semmler treats this as an example of ironic humour—perhaps, but there are some signs of tension behind the controlled exterior. Lindsay spoke of Paterson suffering from nausea in the morning. In 1910 Paterson wrote to Robertson from the country: 'My health is quite restored now. I used not to be able to sleep, now I can't keep awake.'

The property he chose was Coodra Vale at Wee Jasper, about fifty miles east of Yass, a mountainous forty thousand acres with some river flats on the upper reaches of the Murrumbidgee. Paterson afterwards called it hillbilly country and said that 'as a station proposition it was better avoided', but that was hindsight. The original plan was for the property to be purchased by a syndicate of four, but it ended up being a partnership between Paterson and Charles Lindeman, of the Hunter Valley winemaking family. Lindeman, an older man, was something of a success story. When disease destroyed the wine industry a decade earlier, Lindeman had revived it through a one-man sales campaign in London.

Paterson lived at Coodra Vale but running a property requires abilities more diverse than handling horses. The partnership did not succeed. By 1912 Paterson was wheat farming in the northwest of New South Wales, near Grenfell. In the scale of status in the Australian bush,

wheat farming ranked distinctly below running sheep.
By the end of 1912 Paterson was back in Sydney doing
journalism. There were no royalties coming in but he
was working on a manuscript called *Racehorses and
Racing in Australia*, which he was to complete in 1914.
It might have been thought that Robertson would have
published it; even if he had some doubts, surely he owed
something to an author who had made him so much
money and the name of Paterson coupled with horses
must have meant something in sales. But Robertson
rejected the book.

The outbreak of war in 1914 offered Paterson something
of a delivery. Unfortunately for him, the post of Official
War Correspondent (the British had told Australia only
one would be allowed) went to C.E.W. Bean, after a
ballot of Australian Journalists' Association members. In
November 1914 Paterson set out for London, hoping to
reactivate his Boer War contacts, but the War Office didn't
want any more journalists, let alone colonials. Lady
Dudley, the wife of a former Governor-General, whom
Paterson had met in Australia, financed a private hospital
for the wounded in France, staffed by Australian doctors
and nurses. Paterson got himself taken on as an am-
bulance driver, transporting the wounded from trains
to the hospital. He hoped that once in France there
might be an opening for a correspondent, but when it
became evident this wasn't going to happen he returned
to Australia.

At 51 Paterson could hardly hope to go into a fighting
unit, but he found himself a place—in charge of the
Remount Unit in Egypt. In the three years he was there,
roughriders under Major Paterson broke in 50 000 horses
and 10 000 mules. Alice Paterson, along with a number
of other officers' wives, followed him to Cairo. Dame Mabel
Brookes in her memoirs has a story of Paterson, dirty
and dishevelled, striding into the upmarket Shepheards
Hotel to meet his wife. He explained how he and twelve

drivers had broken the rules, taking 200 mules through the streets of Cairo from one side to the other, and claimed to have lost only two, which had fallen into a tomb.

Paterson's only published writings from the war were four not very good poems and four articles on army life published in the local army newspaper, the *Kia-Ora Coo-ee*. In 1917 Angus and Robertson published *Three Elephant Power and Other Stories,* a collection of stories and journalism, as well as a third collection of verse, *Saltbush Bill, J.P. and other Verses*, which included 'Waltzing Matilda' for the first time in a book.

In 1903, in search of cash, Paterson sold copyright of 'Waltzing Matilda' and a few other pieces to his publisher, who the same year sold it on to Inglis Tea. It was set to music and published in sheet music form, a common advertising device directed at all those pianists in the parlour. The verses cropped up again in a widely sold university song book in 1911. It hadn't, however, taken on among the soldiers during the war. A survey in the *Kia-Ora Coo-ee* of troops' preferences didn't mention it: they preferred music hall songs.

On his return to Australia in 1919 Paterson had some royalties from the books published in his absence, but he needed journalism to survive. He wrote for the newly established *Smith's Weekly*, which saw itself as a mouthpiece for the returned soldiers. Paterson took up the cause of the men who wanted to be helped to go on the land. An earlier article from Egypt had told of his interviews with soldiers who wanted to make such a new life. In Australia on his return Paterson wrote critically of bureaucratic bungling and delays in dealing with the returned men—yet another indication of how he should not be categorised as a spokesman for the squatters. Most of the squatters were distrustful of the soldier settlement schemes, fearing that their best land might be taken and also (with some justification) that the blocks would be uneconomic. But here, thirty years on, Paterson was repeating the theme of his 1889 pamphlet, the need to unlock the land.

He wrote another novel called *The Cook's Dog*, but in 1920 Robertson rejected that manuscript. Paterson, with his wife, son and daughter, was living at the time in a modest flat in Edgecliff, in Sydney's eastern suburbs.

In 1921 Paterson was employed as editor of the *Sydney Sportsman*, as well as being appointed to the board of the company which published the journal. The paper, a weekly costing 6d, was founded in 1900 by one of the more bizarre figures of Sydney journalism, John Norton, who was also the proprietor of the weekly journal *Truth*. In his will John Norton had disinherited his only son, Ezra, who had taken his mother's side during violent and vituperative divorce proceedings. When Paterson was appointed to the *Sportsman* the will was under challenge and both papers carried on their mastheads 'Published by John Norton's trustees'. The *Sportsman* was a lively paper, carrying lengthy articles on just about every sport from racing through to rifle shooting. It even ran to reports of dog shows, and drama criticism. As weeklies did in those days, it carried large photographs of sportsmen or the Governor at the races, with sundry committee noteworthies looking solemn. One of Paterson's changes was to introduce photos of 'Bondi Belles', in their costumes, taken by the *Sporstman*'s own photographer. Paterson used the opportunity given by the necessity to fill space to dash off some comic verse. An early example of a punter talking to a barmaid about favourites was signed U.K. Lely, while The Banjo was revived for others. Sometimes they were unsigned, but his style showed through, as in 'Song of a Snob—A Ballad of Class':

> *If I should meet destruction in the town,*
> *Let there be something classy to record,*
> *If any motor car should run me down*
> *Let it not be a Ford.*

I would die content if some Rolls Royce,
Owned by some wealthy and patrician dame,
Whose name would make the inquest really choice,
Blow out my vital flame.

If accident befall me, may the stamp
Of birth and breeding lighten the award.
If some-one jabs my eyes with his gamp,
Oh let it be a Lord!

Not one of the great contributions, just a filler, but nice evidence that Banjo Paterson didn't take himself too seriously.

Moving from part-time to full-time employment meant that Paterson became eligible for membership of his union, the Australian Journalists' Association, which he promptly joined. More than that, he became active, chairing a meeting to establish a writers' union within the AJA 'to regulate and protect conditions and relations between authors and publishers'. When the national body was established a few months later Paterson became the national vice-president, but the organisation petered out. As Robertson's deals had proved over the years, writers in Australia were not in a strong position when it came to negotiation with publishers.

The *Sportsman* carried editorials, and most of them in Paterson's early years as editor bore his mark. When a group of clergymen tried to stop tennis being played on municipal courts on Sundays he upbraided them 'for an attempt to re-establish clerical control over the actions of an enlightened and educated community'. He was a long way ahead of his time in mocking the bogus distinctions between amateur and professional in any sport: '. . . the old amateur definition was introduced by Englishmen to keep out the non-moneyed classes'. He took pleasure in pointing out that the great English cricketers Hobbs and Sutcliffe were professionals. Logically, Paterson called for open Olympics. The man who years ago had written

'Only a Jockey' published a front-page story condemning
the Moorefield Racing Club for still relying on a horse-
drawn ambulance. Even though he ran shooting articles
Paterson argued for bird sanctuaries, chiding New South
Wales for lagging behind Victoria. Headlines could be
frank. In 1922 one story about a race meeting where the
jockey was killed was headed 'A Suicide Meeting—Held
at Mudgee—Crooked Practices Rampant'.

John Norton's will was overturned and his son took
over the company. Paterson was dropped from the board
but stayed on as editor; he also wrote for *Truth*, but his
byline didn't appear there. For Paterson, the man who
mixed in good society, to be associated with a journal
like *Truth* was something of an anomaly. Its staple was
court reporting with the divorce cases providing an ele-
ment of sex. It was not a paper that respectable people
allowed in the house—if it was found, the Sydney joke
went, then the maid had brought it in. Ezra Norton was
an odd boss for the reserved, courtly Paterson. The new
proprietor was a short, unhappy man, consistently foul-
mouthed and a terrible bully; he liked to surround himself
with a sycophantic bodyguard of ex-pugs. But Ezra loved
horses and indeed all animals with a depth of passion
that he did not extend to his fellow human beings. The
horses and the racing world would have been their only
bond, but a strong one. There was something else—Ezra
would have liked the idea that Australia's most celebrated
national poet was on his payroll.

For Paterson editorship of the *Sportsman* was a job
which gave him freedom from the grind of the freelance
and also what he liked best, being with horses. Still, over
the years the character of the paper changed. By the end
of the 1920s it was dominated by racing, the minor sports
getting less space. Stories were shorter and more clipped
in style. Paterson's tone didn't show up in the leaders
and the jokey verse-fillers were no more. One old col-
league of Paterson's recalled that by then he was not

very active in the office. Unfailingly courteous to all, he came in every morning: precisely at noon he stood up and left to go to the races or, if they were not on, to the Australian Club for an afternoon of bridge. In 1930, aged 66, he retired.

Through the thirties he did some journalism, mainly for the *Sydney Morning Herald* and its weekly associate the *Sydney Mail*. There wasn't much money in it. For two articles for the *Herald* in May 1935 he got £9/3/—. It's been said that he wrote for *Smith's Weekly* in this period, but they don't seem to have used his byline.

There would have been a dribble of money from fresh material published after 1908 (when he had sold his previous copyrights) and in 1934 Angus and Robertson published a collection of his Boer War dispatches and travel writings under the title *Happy Dispatches*. As a good bridge player he could expect to make modest amounts for gentlemen's clubs ignored the laws against gambling and he played privately. There is also a suggestion that his wife had some money of her own. He received commissions from buying horses for people and advising them. One man who first met him in the late twenties said to me: 'From the time I knew him, everyone knew that he didn't have a cracker, he'd sold his copyrights for a song'.

Still the Patersons' flat was something of an open house. They entertained widely and there was the inevitable bridge. Of his many friends Paterson was closest to a contrasting pair—Dame Eadith Walker, a philanthropist who never married but was still something of a leader of Sydney society and who probably gave away a million pounds in her life, and A.B. Piddington, an intellectual lawyer, who resigned a judicial position in protest against the dismissal by the State Governor of the Labor Premier Jack Lang. In the early thirties the Patersons moved into a house in Double Bay, still standing, although now much changed.

Was Paterson a gambler? Was that the reason he was not well-off? Certainly he wrote with the ring of experience about betting and Norman Lindsay recalls a wager with him. Still, excess wasn't his style and we really need look no further than his earnings to understand why he was never rich, as he might well have been if he'd persevered with the law. Indeed, betting may well have provided some income—if he took commissions on buying horses it would have been an easy step to placing bets on commission at the track for his friends away in the country. He remained restless at heart, travelling around the country, looking at studs and visiting stations. A lot of properties seem to have been left an inscribed copy of his verse.

By now Paterson had become something of an icon. Children would be introduced to him as to a venerable figure. His wife Alice was a cousin of the Whites and Patrick White remembered that he was eating watermelon in the garden when his grazier father brought along Patrick's first poet:

> He was dressed like other gentlemen in a tobacco-coloured suit and gold watch-chain, trilby hat, and one of those stiff collars which grew grubby at the edges soon after contact with the cleanest skins. This was the driest kind of gentleman, his face like a sooty lemon. My father introduced him as 'Mr' Banjo Paterson. Whether the stranger spoke to a child whose face was buried in a slice of melon, I can't remember. My father seemed proud of their relationship.

Respect was not universal. A.W. José, the man who had beaten him for *The Times* job, and whose sense of humour Paterson had questioned, in a memoir of the nineties put *The Banjo* down, saying his verse was 'almost entirely the product of his holidays and moments off duty'. Literary paybacks often come years later.

In 1934 one of his creations, one that Paterson hardly

cared about, 'Waltzing Matilda', received a boost which was to propel it a very long way. That year a visiting Englishman, Thomas Wood, produced *Cobbers*, a book about Australian life and ways which proved to be an extraordinary bestseller. Wood printed 'Waltzing Matilda' as his frontispiece and said that it should be Australia's unofficial national anthem. There was another reason why Paterson would have been surprised at its being taken up, quite apart from his estimate of its intrinsic worth. It would not have escaped the high-spirited young people clowning around that night in 1895 that there was an element of *double-entendre* in the tag 'Waltzing Matilda', a phrase making a joke about lonely travelling men's lack of women and their need to make do with a swag instead. It was unlikely that the swagmen had ballroom dancing in mind when they were dreaming about women, either. It's a little like all those Irish clergymen who sing 'Tipperary' without realising that the Tipperary in that World War I soldiers' song was in fact a brothel area in London. Paterson would have enjoyed the irony.

He used his talent for light verse again in a collection for children called *The Animals Noah Forgot*, published in 1933, with Norman Lindsay doing what he did best, as the illustrator. There was also another novel, *The Shearer's Colt*, published in 1936, a complicated racing novel with a muddled overweight narrative which didn't sell well.

Paterson had always suffered from asthma and it got worse as he grew older. But he was still a regular at the races, with an accustomed place at Randwick at the end of the members' stand, and carrying an outsize pair of binoculars, the tool of the racing journalist. In 1939, in four long articles in the *Sydney Morning Herald*, he produced the nearest he ever came to an autobiography.

In 1938 Paterson was awarded the CBE. Poets, even national institutions, could not hope for the knighthoods

given to worthy industrialists and politicians. When
Paterson got the third-rate honour, most likely in the
eyes of the kind of people who made decisions on honours
he was seen as a bit of a failure, not on the scale of
Lawson, but a failure nevertheless. Like a sportsman
he had peaked early. As a poet his best work was done
when he was still young. His novels failed. He failed to
become *The Times* correspondent, and he failed as a daily
newspaper editor. His great book on racing was never
published. The writers' union he had set up petered out.
As an editor he had failed a second time and had seen
the paper change from the style he liked best. When he
had gone on the land it had come to nothing. It was
something of an irony that Paterson, the man who spoke
for the bush, spent only twelve of his 77 years living in
the country. In his retirement he did not even have the
security of his own home. It is agreed however, that he
had a happy family life and hosts of friends and there
were the sustaining rituals of the race-watcher: stand-
ing up as the horses moved to the barrier, lifting the
binoculars, focusing on the horses as they burst away
from the start and the follow-through to the climax of
the finish.

In early 1941 he suffered a heart attack and was
hospitalised. He recovered well enough to be discharged
and on 5 February, sitting in the hospital hallway wait-
ing to be picked up, he had another heart attack, this
time fatal. The obituaries gave due praise with stress on
the positive aspects of his work, making an unstated
comparison with Lawson. In doing so they were echoing
the way his publishers had sold Paterson to a new gen-
eration. The dustjackets of the editions of *Collected Verse*
during the thirties carried the message:

> Mr A.B. Paterson is a cheerful poet. He looks on
> life as a banquet to which he has been bidden
> and welcomed, and to which he brings a good
> appetite. He is a good 'sport' who has grown up

among the places he describes . . . he sees and feels the Beauty of Australia, spontaneously that no effort of art is apparent in his work.

Such a sales pitch flattered bluff, honest Australians that this was one book of poetry they need not feel ashamed to buy. Paterson, however, was a more complex man than a mere merry juggler of words. We don't have to make pretentious claims for his verse; Paterson never did himself. For a time his verse authentically articulated an Australia that even then was passing. When we understand 'On Kiley's Run', we can know that Paterson was far from always being cheerful. When he was prepared to coolly label Kipling, a man he admired for other things, as a carpetbagger at the war, when he was prepared to report the other side from Olive Schreiner or to note how wounded English officers got more attention than their soldiers, he was not being cheerful. When given the chance he was more than just a reporter with an acute eye and ear. Even so, for all his capacity for seriousness, he *was* the supreme practitioner of comic verse.

Banjo Paterson has always been worth reading and always will be worth reading.

Notes on selection

All anthologies are personal. Anyone like myself bought up on a battered copy of the old *Collected Verse*, with the front cover detached by constant use, has accumulated a formidable list of favourites which makes the process of selection easier. I have chosen to group the ballads and the prose in themes, because I think chronological or alphabetical solutions scramble things. Some ballads dropped by other anthologists have been restored. I have put back 'The Boss of the *Admiral Lynch*', which used to move me very much, I suspect because I like lost causes; one suspects that behind his stoic facade Paterson did too. When he wrote about the death of Gilbert the bushranger, cornered but going out fighting, Paterson the gentleman rider was rather more on the side of the outcast than his respectable readers would care to admit. Indeed, sometimes the outsider does win, not only on the racetrack but in life. Saltbush Bill, the King of the Outback, scores not by pluck but by cunning.

In prose Paterson's reputation has been smothered by the dull, sanitised collection in *Happy Dispatches*, put out in 1934 when he needed the money. Much of his journalism was, as is the nature of things, ephemeral, but when he had the opportunity, either at a dog-fight in the sandhills or on a stony ridge under fire, Paterson was a very good reporter. His actual dispatches from the Boer War as they were published at the time merit him a place with the best of war correspondents. His travel writing tended to be crippled by the curse of the English essayists' editorialising style. However, 'An Informal

Letter from London' is good for its unsentimental view of the English connection, probably the only time that tone was taken in the *Sydney Morning Herald* for decades before or after.

In fiction, alas, Paterson lacked narrative skills and his sardonic humour was lost under leaden plots even in the stories. Despite that, I have included one extract from *An Outback Marriage*, where Paterson engages in one of his favourite occupations, sending up the English new-chum.

His last reminiscences, published in 1939, while those of an old man, have the candour and freshness of youth. They are generous memoirs. While he knocks the myth of the martyr Morant, he still strives to understand the man. Paterson will always be remembered for his ballads more than his prose, while with Lawson it is the other way round. The pity of it was that the decline of the *Bulletin* and the intellectual poverty of the press meant that Paterson lacked the opportunity to develop as a prose writer.

Note: There were in many cases more than one version of the poems and stories published over the years; the versions printed here are the later ones. Dates of first publication are also noted.

The Man from Snowy River and Other Verses is referred to as *The Man from Snowy River*; *Rio Grande's Last Race and Other Verses* is referred to as *Rio Grande's Last Race*; likewise *Saltbush Bill, J.P. and Other Verses* is shortened to *Saltbush Bill, J.P.*

The Bush

*. . . the vision splendid of the sunlit plains extended
And at night the wondrous glory of the everlasting
   stars.*

The Man from Snowy River

There was movement at the station, for the word
    had passed around
  That the colt from old Regret had got away,
And had joined the wild bush horses—he was worth
    a thousand pound,
  So all the cracks had gathered to the fray.
All the tried and noted riders from the stations near
    and far
  Had mustered at the homestead overnight,
For the bushmen love hard riding where the wild
    bush horses are,
  And the stock-horse snuffs the battle with delight.

There was Harrison, who made his pile when Pardon
    won the cup,
  The old man with his hair as white as snow;
But few could ride beside him when his blood was
    fairly up—
  He would go wherever horse and man could go.
And Clancy of the Overflow down to lend a
    hand,
  No better horseman ever held the reins;
For never horse could throw him while the saddle-
    girths would stand—
He learnt to ride while droving on the plains.

And one was there, a stripling on a small and weedy
    beast;
  He was something like a racehorse undersized,
With a touch of Timor pony—three parts thorough-
    bred at least—
  And such as are by mountain horsemen prized.

He was hard and tough and wiry—just the sort that
 won't say die—
 There was courage in his quick impatient tread;
And he bore the badge of gameness in his bright
 and fiery eye,
 And the proud and lofty carriage of his head.

But still so slight and weedy, one would doubt his
 power to stay,
 And the old man said, 'That horse will never do
For a long and tiring gallop—lad, you'd better stop
 away,
 Those hills are far too rough for such as you.'
So he waited, sad and wistful—only Clancy stood
 his friend—
 'I think we ought to let him come,' he said;
'I warrant he'll be with us when he's wanted at
 the end,
 For both his horse and he are mountain bred.

'He hails from Snowy River, up by Kosciusko's
 side,
 Where the hills are twice as steep and twice as
 rough;
Where a horse's hoofs strike firelight from the
 flint stones every stride,
 The man that holds his own is good enough.
And the Snowy River riders on the mountains
 make their home,
 Where the river runs those giant hills between;
I have seen full many horsemen since I first com-
 menced to roam,
 But nowhere yet such horsemen have I seen.'

So he went; they found the horses by the big
 mimosa clump,
 They raced away towards the mountain's brow,

And the old man gave his orders, 'Boys, go at
    them from the jump,
  No use to try for fancy riding now.
And, Clancy, you must wheel them, try and wheel
    them to the right.
  Ride boldly, lad, and never fear the spills,
For never yet was rider that could keep the mob
    in sight,
  If once they gain the shelter of those hills.'

So Clancy rode to wheel them—he was racing on
    the wing
  Where the best and boldest riders take their place,
And he raced his stock-horse past them, and he
    made the ranges ring
  With the stockwhip, as he met them face to face.
Then they halted for a moment, while he swung
    the dreaded lash,
  But they saw their well-loved mountain full in
    view,
And they charged beneath the stockwhip with a
    sharp and sudden dash,
  And off into the mountain scrub they flew.

Then fast the horsemen followed, where the gorges
    deep and black
  Resounded to the thunder of their tread,
And the stockwhips woke the echoes, and they
    fiercely answered back
  From cliffs and crags that beetled overhead.
And upward, ever upward, the wild horses held
    their way,
  Where mountain ash and kurrajong grew wide;
And the old man muttered fiercely, 'We may bid
    the mob good day,
  No man can hold them down the other side.'

When they reached the mountain's summit, even
    Clancy took a pull—
  It well might make the boldest hold their breath;
The wild hop scrub grew thickly, and the hidden
    ground was full
  Of wombat holes, and any slip was death.
But the man from Snowy River let the pony have
    his head,
  And he swung his stockwhip round and gave a
    cheer,
And he raced him down the mountain like a torrent
    down its bed,
  While the others stood and watched in very fear.

He sent the flint-stones flying, but the pony kept his
    feet,
  He cleared the fallen timber in his stride,
And the man from Snowy River never shifted in his
    seat—
  It was grand to see that mountain horseman ride.

Through the stringy barks and saplings, on the
    rough and broken ground,
  Down the hillside at a racing pace he went;
And he never drew the bridle till he landed safe
    and sound
  At the bottom of that terrible descent.

He was right among the horses as they climbed
    the farther hill,
  And the watchers on the mountain, standing mute,
Saw him ply the stockwhip fiercely; he was right
    among them still,
  As he raced across the clearing in pursuit.
Then they lost him for a moment, where two moun-
    tain gullies met
  In the ranges—but a final glimpse reveals
On a dim and distant hillside the wild horses racing
    yet,
  With the man from Snowy River at their heels.

And he ran them single-handed till their sides were
        white with foam;
    He followed like a bloodhound on their track,
Till they halted, cowed and beaten; then he turned
        their heads for home,
    And alone and unassisted brought them back.
But his hardy mountain pony he could scarcely raise
        a trot,
    He was blood from hip to shoulder from the
        spur;
But his pluck was still undaunted, and his courage
        fiery hot,
    For never yet was mountain horse a cur.

And down by Kosciusko, where the pine-clad ridges
        raise
    Their torn and rugged battlements on high,
Where the air is clear as crystal, and the white
        stars fairly blaze
    At midnight in the cold and frosty sky,
And where around the Overflow the reed-beds sweep
        and sway
    To the breezes, and the rolling plains are wide,
The Man from Snowy River is a household word
        to-day,
    And the stockmen tell the story of his ride.

Bulletin, 26 April 1890

CLANCY OF THE OVERFLOW

I had written him a letter which I had, for want of
        better
    Knowledge, sent to where I met him down the
    Lachlan, years ago;

He was shearing when I knew him, so I sent the
    letter to him,
  Just on spec, addressed as follows, 'Clancy, of
    The Overflow'.

And an answer came directed in a writing unex-
    pected
  (And I think the same was written with a thumb-
    nail dipped in tar);
'Twas his shearing mate who wrote it, and *verbatim*
    I will quote it:
'Clancy's gone to Queensland droving, and we
    don't know where he are.'

• • •

In my wild erratic fancy visions come to me of
    Clancy
  Gone a-droving 'down the Cooper' where the
    Western drovers go;
As the stock are slowly stringing, Clancy rides
    behind them singing,
  For the drover's life has pleasures that the towns-
    folk never know.

And the bush has friends to meet him, and their
    kindly voices greet him
  In the murmur of the breezes and the river on
    its bars,
And he sees the vision splendid of the sunlit plains
    extended,
  And at night the wondrous glory of the ever-
    lasting stars.

• • •

I am sitting in my dingy little office, where a stingy
  Ray of sunlight struggles feebly down between
    the houses tall,
And the foetid air and gritty of the dusty, dirty city,
  Through the open window floating, spreads its
    foulness over all.

And in place of lowing cattle, I can hear the fiendish
    rattle
    Of the tramways and the buses making hurry
    down the street;
And the language uninviting of the gutter children
    fighting
    Comes fitfully and faintly through the ceaseless
    tramp of feet.

And the hurrying people daunt me, and their pallid
    faces haunt me
    As they shoulder one another in their rush and
    nervous haste,
With their eager eyes and greedy, and their stunted
    forms and weedy,
    For townsfolk have no time to grow, they have
    no time to waste.

And I somehow rather fancy that I'd like to change
    with Clancy,
    Like to take a turn at droving where the seasons
    come and go,
While he faced the round eternal of the cash-book
    and the journal—
    But I doubt he'd suit the office, Clancy, of The
    Overflow.

Bulletin, 21 December 1889

CONROY'S GAP

This was the way of it, don't you know—
    Ryan was 'wanted' for stealing sheep,
And never a trooper, high or low,
    Could find him—catch a weasel asleep!

Till Trooper Scott, from the Stockman's Ford—
  A bushman, too, as I've heard them tell—
Chanced to find him drunk as a lord
  Round at the Shadow of Death Hotel.

D'you know the place? It's a wayside inn,
  A low grog-shanty—a bushman trap,
Hiding away in its shame and sin
  Under the shelter of Conroy's Gap—
Under the shade of that frowning range
  The roughest crowd that ever drew breath—
Thieves and rowdies, uncouth and strange,
  Were mustered round at the 'Shadow of Death'.

The trooper knew that his man would slide
  Like a dingo pup, if he saw the chance;
And with half a start on the mountain side
  Ryan would lead him a merry dance.
Drunk as he was when the trooper came,
  To him that did not matter a rap—
Drunk or sober, he was the same,
  The boldest rider in Conroy's Gap.

'I want you, Ryan,' the trooper said,
  'And listen to me, if you dare resist,
So help me heaven, I'll shoot you dead!'
  He snapped the steel on his prisoner's wrist,
And Ryan, hearing the handcuffs click,
  Recovered his wits as they turned to go,
For fright will sober a man as quick
  As all the drugs that the doctors know.

There was a girl in that shanty bar
  Went by the name of Kate Carew,
Quiet and shy as the bush girls are,
  But ready-witted and plucky, too.

She loved this Ryan, or so they say,
  And passing by, while her eyes were dim
With tears, she said in a careless way,
  'The Swagman's round in the stable, Jim.'

Spoken too low for the trooper's ear,
  Why should she care if he heard or not?
Plenty of swagmen far and near—
  And yet to Ryan it meant a lot.
That was the name of the grandest horse
  In all the district from east to west;
In every show ring, on every course,
  They always counted The Swagman best.

He was a wonder, a raking bay—
  One of the grand old Snowdon strain—
One of the sort that could race and stay,
  With his mighty limbs and his length of rein.
Born and bred on the mountain side,
  He could race through scrub like a kangaroo;
The girl herself on his back might ride,
  And The Swagman would carry her safely
    through.

He would travel gaily from daylight's flush
  Till after the stars hung out their lamps;
There was never his like in the open bush,
  And never his match on the cattle-camps
For faster horses might well be found
  On racing tracks, or a plain's extent,
But few, if any, on broken ground
  Could see the way that The Swagman went.

When this girl's father, old Jim Carew,
  Was droving out on the Castlereagh
With Conroy's cattle, a wire came through
  To say that his wife couldn't live the day.
And he was a hundred miles from home,
  As flies the crow, with never a track

Through plains as pathless as ocean's foam;
   He mounted straight on The Swagman's back.

He left the camp by the sundown light,
   And the settlers out on the Marthaguy
Awoke and heard, in the dead of night,
   A single horseman hurrying by.
He crossed the Bogan at Dandaloo,
   And many a mile of the silent plain
That lonely rider behind him threw
   Before they settled to sleep again.

He rode all night, and he steered his course
   By the shining stars with a bushman's skill,
And every time he pressed his horse
   The Swagman answered him gamely still.
He neared his home as the east was bright,
   The doctor met him outside the town:
'Carew! How far did you come last night?'
   'A hundred miles since the sun went down.'

And his wife got round, and an oath he passed,
   So long as he or one of his breed
Could raise a coin, though it was their last
   The Swagman never should want a feed.
And Kate Carew, when her father died,
   She kept the horse and she kept him well:
The pride of the district far and wide,
   He lived in style at the bush hotel.

Such was The Swagman; and Ryan knew
   Nothing about could pace the crack;
Little he'd care for the man in blue
   If once he got on The Swagman's back.
But how to do it? A word let fall
   Gave him the hint as the girl passed by;
Nothing but 'Swagman—stable wall;
   Go to the stable and mind your eye.'

He caught her meaning, and quickly turned
    To the trooper: 'Reckon you'll gain a stripe
By arresting me, and it's easily earned;
    Let's go to the stable and get my pipe,
The Swagman has it.' So off they went,
    And as soon as ever they turned their backs
The girl slipped down, on some errand bent
    Behind the stable, and seized an axe.

The trooper stood at the stable door
    While Ryan went in quite cool and slow,
And then (the trick had been played before)
    The girl outside gave the wall a blow.
Three slabs fell out of the stable wall—
    'Twas done 'fore ever the trooper knew—
And Ryan, as soon as he saw them fall,
    Mounted The Swagman and rushed him through.

The trooper heard the hoofbeats ring
    In the stable yard, and he slammed the gate,
But The Swagman rose with a mighty spring
    At the fence, and the trooper fired too late,
As they raced away, and his shots flew wide
    And Ryan no longer need care a rap,
For never a horse that was lapped in hide
    Could catch The Swagman in Conroy's Gap.

And that's the story. You want to know
    If Ryan came back to his Kate Carew;
Of course he should have, as stories go,
    But the worst of it is, this story's true;
And in real life it's a certain rule,
    Whatever the poets and authors say
Of high-toned robbers and all their school,
    These horse thief fellows aren't built that
        way.

Come back! Don't hope it—the slinking
  hound,
  He sloped across to the Queensland side,
And sold The Swagman for fifty pound,
  And stole the money, and more beside.
And took to drink, and by some good chance
  Was killed—thrown out of a stolen trap.
And that was the end of this small romance,
  The end of the story of Conroy's Gap.

Bulletin, 20 December 1890

THE TRAVELLING POST OFFICE

The roving breezes come and go, the reed-beds
  sweep and sway,
The sleepy river murmurs low, and loiters on its
  way,
It is the land of lots o' time along the Castlereagh.

•   •   •

The old man's son had left the farm, he found it
  dull and slow,
He drifted to the great North-west, where all the
  rovers go.
'He's gone so long,' the old man said, 'he's dropped
  right out of mind,
But if you'd write a line to him I'd take it very
  kind;
He's shearing here and fencing there, a kind of
  waif and stray—
He's droving now with Conroy's sheep along the
  Castlereagh.

'The sheep are travelling for the grass, and travel-
    ling very slow;
They may be at Mundooran now, or past the Over-
    flow,
Or tramping down the black-soil flats across by
    Waddiwong;
But all those little country towns would send the
    letter wrong.
The mailman, if he's extra tired, would pass them
    in his sleep;
It's safest to address the note to "Care of Conroy's
    sheep",
For five and twenty thousand head can scarcely
    go astray,
You write to "Care of Conroy's sheep along the
    Castlereagh".'

By rock and ridge and riverside the western mail
    has gone
Across the great Blue Mountain Range to take that
    letter on.
A moment on the topmast grade, while open fire-
    doors glare,
She pauses like a living thing to breathe the moun-
    tain air,
Then launches down the other side across the plains
    away
To bear that note to 'Conroy's sheep along the
    Castlereagh'.

And now by coach and mailman's bag it goes from
    town to town,
And Conroy's Gap and Conroy's Creek have marked
    it 'Further down'.
Beneath a sky of deepest blue, where never cloud
    abides,

A speck upon the waste of plain the lonely mail-
    man rides.
Where fierce hot winds have set the pine and myall
    boughs asweep
He hails the shearers passing by for news of
    Conroy's sheep.
By big lagoons where wildfowl play and crested
    pigeons flock,
By camp-fires where the drovers ride around their
    restless stock,
And past the teamster toiling down to fetch the
    wool away
My letter chases Conroy's sheep along the Castle-
    reagh.

Bulletin, 10 March 1894

In the Droving Days

'Only a pound,' said the auctioneer,
'Only a pound; and I'm standing here
Selling this animal, gain or loss—
Only a pound for the drover's horse?
One of the sort that was ne'er afraid,
One of the boys of the Old Brigade;
Thoroughly honest and game, I'll swear,
Only a little the worse for wear;
Plenty as bad to be seen in town,
Give me a bid and I'll knock him down;
Sold as he stands, and without recourse,
Give me a bid for the drover's horse.'

Loitering there in an aimless way
Somehow I noticed the poor old grey,
Weary and battered and screwed, of course;
Yet when I noticed the old grey horse,

The rough bush saddle, and single rein
Of the bridle laid on his tangled mane,
Straightway the crowd and the auctioneer
Seemed on a sudden to disappear,
Melted away in a kind of haze—
For my heart went back to the droving days.

Back to the road, and I crossed again
Over the miles of the saltbush plain—
The shining plain that is said to be
The dried-up bed of an inland sea,
Where the air so dry and so clear and bright
Refracts the sun with a wondrous light,
And out in the dim horizon makes
The deep blue gleam of the phantom lakes.

At dawn of day we could feel the breeze
That stirred the boughs of the sleeping trees,
And brought a breath of the fragrance rare
That comes and goes in that scented air;
For the trees and grass and the shrubs contain
A dry sweet scent on the saltbush plain.
For those that love it and understand
The saltbush plain is a wonderland,
A wondrous country, where Nature's ways
Were revealed to me in the droving days.

We saw the fleet wild horses pass,
And the kangaroos through the Mitchell grass;
The emu ran with her frightened brood
All unmolested and unpursued.
But there rose a shout and a wild hubbub
When the dingo raced for his native scrub,
And he paid right dear for his stolen meals
With the drover's dogs at his wretched heels.
For we ran him down at a rattling pace,
While the pack-horse joined in the stirring chase.
And a wild halloo at the kill we'd raise—
We were light of heart in the droving days.

'Twas a drover's horse, and my hand again
Made a move to close on a fancied rein.
For I felt the swing and the easy stride
Of the grand old horse that I used to ride.
In drought or plenty, in good or ill,
The same old steed was my comrade still;
The old grey horse with his honest ways
Was a mate to me in the droving days.

When we kept our watch in the cold and damp,
If the cattle broke from the sleeping camp,
Over the flats and across the plain,
With my head bent down on his waving mane,
Through the boughs above and the stumps below,
On the darkest night I could let him go
At a racing speed; he would choose his course,
And my life was safe with the old grey horse.
But man and horse had a favourite job,
When an outlaw broke from a station mob;
With a right good will was the stockwhip plied,
As the old horse raced at the straggler's side,
And the greenhide whip such a weal would raise—
We could use the whip in the droving days.

•   •   •

'Only a pound!' and was this the end—
Only a pound for the drover's friend.
The drover's friend that had seen his day,
And now was worthless and cast away
With a broken knee and a broken heart
To be flogged and starved in a hawker's cart.
Well, I made a bid for a sense of shame
And the memories dear of the good old game.

'Thank you? Guinea! and cheap at that!
Against you there in the curly hat!
Only a guinea, and one more chance,
Down he goes if there's no advance,

Third, and the last time, one! two! three!'
And the old grey horse was knocked down to me.
And now he's wandering, fat and sleek,
On the lucerne flats by the Homestead Creek;
I dare not ride him for fear he'd fall,
But he does a journey to beat them all,
For though he scarcely a trot can raise,
He can take me back to the droving days.

Bulletin, 20 June 1891

ON KILEY'S RUN

The roving breezes come and go
          On Kiley's Run,
The sleepy river murmurs low,
And far away one dimly sees
Beyond the stretch of forest trees—
Beyond the foothills dusk and dun—
The ranges sleeping in the sun
          On Kiley's Run.

'Tis many years since first I came
          To Kiley's Run,
More years than I would care to name
Since I, a stripling, used to ride
For miles and miles at Kiley's side,
The while in stirring tones he told
The stories of the days of old
          On Kiley's Run.

I see the old bush homestead now
          On Kiley's Run,
Just nestled down beneath the brow

Of one small ridge above the sweep
Of river-flat, where willows weep
And jasmine flowers and roses bloom:
The air was laden with perfume
      On Kiley's Run.

We lived the good old station life
      On Kiley's Run,
With little thought of care or strife.
Old Kiley seldom used to roam,
He liked to make the Run his home;
The swagman never turned away
With empty hand at close of day
      From Kiley's Run.

We kept a racehorse now and then
      On Kiley's Run,
And neighbouring stations brought their men
To meetings where the sport was free,
And dainty ladies came to see
Their champions ride; with laugh and song
The old house rang the whole night long
      On Kiley's Run.

The station-hands were friends, I wot,
      On Kiley's Run,
A reckless, merry-hearted lot—
All splendid riders, and they knew
The boss was kindness through and through.
Old Kiley always stood their friend,
And so they served him to the end
      On Kiley's Run.

But droughts and losses came apace
      To Kiley's Run,
Till ruin stared him in the face;
He toiled and toiled while lived the light,
He dreamed of overdrafts at night:

At length, because he could not pay,
His bankers took the stock away
       From Kiley's Run.

Old Kiley stood and saw them go
       From Kiley's Run.
The well-bred cattle marching slow;
His stockmen, mates for many a day,
They wrung his hand and went away.
Too old to make another start,
Old Kiley died—of broken heart,
       On Kiley's Run.

     •   •   •

The owner lives in England now
       Of Kiley's Run.
He knows a racehorse from a cow;
But that is all he knows of stock:
His chiefest care is how to dock
Expenses, and he sends from town
To cut the shearers' wages down
       On Kiley's Run.

There are no neighbours anywhere
       Near Kiley's Run.
The hospitable homes are bare,
The gardens gone; for no pretence
Must hinder cutting down expense;
The homestead that we held so dear
Contains a half-paid overseer
       On Kiley's Run.

All life and sport and hope have died
       On Kiley's Run.
No longer there the stockmen ride;
For sour-faced boundary riders creep
On mongrel horses after sheep,

Through ranges where, at racing speed,
Old Kiley used to 'wheel the lead'
  On Kiley's Run.

There runs a lane for thirty miles
  Through Kiley's Run.
On either side the herbage smiles,
But wretched travelling sheep must pass
Without a drink or blade of grass
Through that long lane of death and shame:
The weary drovers curse the name
  Of Kiley's Run.

The name itself is changed of late
  Of Kiley's Run.
They call it 'Chandos Park Estate'.
The lonely swagman through the dark
Must hump his swag past Chandos Park—
The name is English, don't you see;
The old name sweeter sounds to me
  Of Kiley's Run.

I cannot guess what fate will bring
  To Kiley's Run—
For chances come and changes ring—
I scarcely think 'twill always be
Locked up to suit an absentee;
And if he lets it out in farms
His tenants soon will carry arms
  On Kiley's Run.

   Bulletin, 20 December 1890

UNDER THE SHADOW OF KILEY'S HILL

This is the place where they all were bred;
 Some of the rafters are standing still;

Now they are scattered and lost and dead,
Every one from the old nest fled,
   Out of the shadow of Kiley's Hill.

Better it is that they ne'er came back—
   Changes and chances are quickly rung;
Now the old homestead is gone to rack,
Green is the grass on the well-worn track
   Down by the gate where the roses clung.

Gone is the garden they kept with care;
   Left to decay at its own sweet will,
Fruit-trees and flower-beds eaten bare,
Cattle and sheep where the roses were,
   Under the shadow of Kiley's Hill.

Where are the children that strove and grew
   In the old homestead in days gone by?
One is away on the far Barcoo
Watching his cattle the long year through,
   Watching them starve in the droughts and die.

One, in the town where all cares are rife,
   Weary with troubles that cramp and kill,
Fain would be done with the restless strife,
Fain would go back to the old bush life,
   Back to the shadow of Kiley's Hill.

One is away on the roving quest,
   Seeking his share of the golden spoil;
Out in the wastes of the trackless west,
Wandering ever he gives the best
   Of his years and strength to the hopeless toil.

What of the parents? That unkept mound
   Shows where they slumber united still;

Rough is their grave, but they sleep as sound
Out on the range as in holy ground,
  Under the shadow of Kiley's Hill.

The Man from Snowy River, 1895

'HE GIVETH HIS BELOVED SLEEP'

The long day passes with its load of sorrow:
  In slumber deep
I lay me down to rest until to-morrow—
  Thank God for sleep.

Thank God for all respite from weary toiling,
  From cares that creep
Across our lives like evil shadows, spoiling
  God's kindly sleep.

We plough and sow, and, as the hours grow later,
  We strive to reap,
And build our barns, and hope to build them greater
  Before we sleep.

We toil and strain and strive with one another
  In hopes to heap
Some greater share of profit than our brother
  Before we sleep.

What will it profit that with tears or laughter
  Our watch we keep?
Beyond it all there lies the Great Hereafter!
  Thank God for sleep!

For, at the last, beseeching Christ to save us,
    We turn with deep
Heart-felt thanksgiving unto God, who gave us
The Gift of Sleep.

Rio Grande's Last Race, 1902

A MOUNTAIN STATION

I bought a run a while ago
    On country rough and ridgy,
Where wallaroos and wombats grow—
    The Upper Murrumbidgee.
The grass is rather scant, it's true,
    But this a fair exchange is,
The sheep can see a lovely view
    By climbing up the ranges.

And She-oak Flat's the station's name,
    I'm not surprised at that, sirs:
The oaks were there before I came,
    And I supplied the flat, sirs.
A man would wonder how it's done,
    The stock so soon decreases—
They sometimes tumble off the run
    And break themselves to pieces.

I've tried to make expenses meet,
    But wasted all my labours;
The sheep the dingoes didn't eat
    Were stolen by the neighbours.
They stole my pears—my native pears—
    Those thrice-convicted felons,
And ravished from me unawares
    My crop of paddy-melons.

And sometimes under sunny skies,
  Without an explanation,
The Murrumbidgee used to rise
  And overflow the station.
But this was caused (as now I know)
  When summer sunshine glowing
Had melted all Kiandra's snow
  And set the river going.

Then in the news, perhaps, you read:
  'Stock Passings. Puckawidgee,
Fat cattle: Seven hundred head
  Swept down the Murrumbidgee;
Their destination's quite obscure,
  But, somehow, there's a notion,
Unless the river falls, they're sure
  To reach the Southern Ocean.'

So after that I'll give it best;
  No more with Fate I'll battle.
I'll let the river take the rest,
  For those were all my cattle.
And with one comprehensive curse
  I close my brief narration,
And advertise it in my verse—
  'For Sale! A Mountain Station.'

Bulletin, 19 December 1891

BLACK SWANS

As I lie at rest on a patch of clover
In the Western Park when the day is done,

I watch as the wild black swans fly over
With their phalanx turned to the sinking sun;
And I hear the clang of their leader crying
To a lagging mate in the rearward flying,
And they fade away in the darkness dying,
Where the stars are mustering one by one.

O ye wild black swans, 'twere a world of wonder
For a while to join in your westward flight,
With the stars above and the dim earth under,
Through the cooling air of the glorious night.
As we swept along on our pinions winging,
We should catch the chime of a church-bell ringing,
Or the distant note of a torrent singing,
Or the far-off flash of a station light.

From the northern lakes with the reeds and rushes,
Where the hills are clothed with a purple haze,
Where the bell-birds chime and the songs of thrushes
Make music sweet in the jungle maze,
They will hold their course to the westward ever,
Till they reach the banks of the old grey river,
Where the waters wash, and the reed-beds quiver
In the burning heat of the summer days.

O ye strange wild birds, will ye bear a greeting
To the folk that live in that western land?
Then for every sweep of your pinions beating
Ye shall bear a wish to the sunburnt band,
To the stalwart men who are stoutly fighting
With the heat and drought and the dust-storm
        smiting,
Yet whose life somehow has a strange inviting,
When once to the work they have put their hand.

Facing it yet! O my friend stout-hearted,
What does it matter for rain or shine,

For the hopes deferred and the gain departed?
Nothing could conquer that heart of thine.
And thy health and strength are beyond confessing
As the only joys that are worth possessing.
May the days to come be as rich in blessing
As the days we spent in the auld lang syne.

I would fain go back to the old grey river,
To the old bush days when our hearts were light;
But, alas! those days they have fled for ever,
They are like the swans that have swept from
        sight.
And I know full well that the strangers' faces
Would meet us now in our dearest places;
For our day is dead and has left no traces
But the thoughts that live in my mind to-night.

There are folk long dead, and our hearts would
        sicken—
We should grieve for them with a bitter pain;
If the past could live and the dead could quicken,
We then might turn to that life again.
But on lonely nights we should hear them calling,
We should hear their steps on the pathways falling,
We should loathe the life with a hate appalling
In our lonely rides by the ridge and plain.

·   ·   ·

In the silent park is a scent of clover,
And the distant roar of the town is dead,
And I hear once more, as the swans fly over,
Their far-off clamour from overhead.
They are flying west, by their instinct guided,
And for man likewise is his fate decided,
And griefs apportioned and joys divided
By a mighty power with a purpose dread.

The Man from Snowy River, 1895

A BUSHMAN'S SONG

I'm travellin' down the Castlereagh, and I'm a
    station hand,
I'm handy with the ropin' pole, I'm handy with
    the brand,
And I can ride a rowdy colt, or swing the axe
    all day,
But there's no demand for a station hand along
    the Castlereagh.

So it's shift, boys, shift, for there isn't the
      slightest doubt
That we've got to make a shift to the stations
      further out,
With the pack-horse runnin' after, for he
      follows like a dog,
We must strike across the country at the old
      jig-jog.

This old black horse I'm riding—if you'll notice
    what's his brand,
He wears the crooked R, you see—none better in
    the land.
He takes a lot of beatin', and the other day we
    tried,
For a bit of a joke, with a racing bloke, for twenty
    pound aside.

It was shift, boys, shift, for there wasn't the
      slightest doubt
That I had to make him shift, for the money was
      nearly out;
But he cantered home a winner, with the other
      one at the flog—
He's a red-hot sort to pick up with his old
      jig-jog.

I asked a cove for shearin' once along the
    Marthaguy;
'We shear non-union here,' says he. 'I call it
    scab,' says I.
I looked along the shearin' floor before I turned
    to go—
There were eight or ten dashed Chinaman a-shearin'
    in a row.

It was shift, boys, shift, for there wasn't the
    slightest doubt
It was time to make a shift with the leprosy about.
So I saddled up my horses, and I whistled to my
    dog,
And I left his scabby station at the old jig-jog.

I went to Illawarra, where my brother's got a farm,
He has to ask his landlord's leave before he lifts
    his arm:
The landlord owns the countryside—man, woman,
    dog, and cat,
They haven't the cheek to dare to speak without
    they touch their hat.

It was shift, boys, shift, for there wasn't the
    slightest doubt
Their little landlord god and I would soon have
    fallen out;
Was I to touch my hat to him?—was I his bloomin'
    dog?
So I makes for up the country at the old jig-jog.

But it's time that I was movin', I've a mighty way
    to go
Till I drink artesian water from a thousand feet
    below;

Till I meet the overlanders with the cattle comin'
    down,
And I'll work a while till I make a pile, then have
    a spree in town.

So, it's shift, boys, shift, for there isn't the slightest
    doubt
We've got to make a shift to the stations further
    out;
The pack-horse runs behind us, for he follows like
    a dog,
And we cross a lot of country at the old jig-jog.

Bulletin, 24 December 1892

HOW GILBERT DIED

There's never a stone at the sleeper's head,
    There's never a fence beside,
And the wandering stock on the grave may tread
    Unnoticed and undenied;
But the smallest child on the Watershed
    Can tell you how Gilbert died.

For he rode at dusk with his comrade Dunn
    To the hut at the Stockman's Ford;
In the waning light of the sinking sun
    They peered with a fierce accord.
They were outlaws both—and on each man's head
    Was a thousand pounds reward.

They had taken toll of the country round,
    And the troopers came behind
With a black who tracked like a human hound
    In the scrub and the ranges blind:
He could run the trail where a white man's eye
    No sign of a track could find.

He had hunted them out of the One Tree Hill
  And over the Old Man Plain,
But they wheeled their tracks with a wild beast's
    skill,
  And they made for the range again;
Then away to the hut where their grandsire dwelt
  They rode with a loosened rein.

And their grandsire gave them a greeting bold:
  'Come in and rest in peace,
No safer place does the country hold—
  With the night pursuit must cease,
And we'll drink success to the roving boys,
  And to hell with the black police.'

But they went to death when they entered there
  In the hut at the Stockman's Ford,
For their grandsire's words were as false as fair—
  They were doomed to the hangman's cord.
He had sold them both to the black police
  For the sake of the big reward.

In the depth of night there are forms that glide
  As stealthy as serpents creep,
And around the hut where the outlaws hide
  They plant in the shadows deep,
And they wait till the first faint flush of dawn
  Shall waken their prey from sleep.

But Gilbert wakes while the night is dark—
  A restless sleeper aye.
He has heard the sound of a sheep-dog's bark,
  And his horse's warning neigh,
And he says to his mate, 'There are hawks abroad,
  And it's time that we went away.'

Their rifles stood at the stretcher head,
  Their bridles lay to hand;

They wakened the old man out of his bed,
  When they heard the sharp command:
'In the name of the Queen lay down your arms,
  Now, Dunn and Gilbert, stand!'

Then Gilbert reached for his rifle true
  That close at hand he kept;
He pointed straight at the voice, and drew,
  But never a flash outleapt,
For the water ran from the rifle breech—
  It was drenched while the outlaws slept.

Then he dropped the piece with a bitter oath,
  And he turned to his comrade Dunn:
'We are sold,' he said, 'we are dead men both!—
  Still, there may be a chance for one;
I'll stop and I'll fight with the pistol here,
  You take to your heels and run.'

So Dunn crept out on his hands and knees
  In the dim, half-dawning light,
And he made his way to a patch of trees,
  And was lost in the black of night;
And the trackers hunted his tracks all day,
  But they never could trace his flight.

But Gilbert walked from the open door
  In a confident style and rash;
He heard at his side the rifles roar,
  And he heard the bullets crash.
But he laughed as he lifted his pistol-hand,
  And he fired at the rifle flash.

Then out of the shadows the troopers aimed
  At his voice and the pistol sound.
With rifle flashes the darkness flamed—
  He staggered and spun around,

And they riddled his body with rifle balls
   As it lay on the blood-soaked ground.

There's never a stone at the sleeper's head,
   There's never a fence beside,
And the wandering stock on the grave may tread
   Unnoticed and undenied;
But the smallest child on the Watershed
   Can tell you how Gilbert died.

Bulletin, 2 June 1894

COME-BY-CHANCE

As I pondered very weary o'er a volume long and
      dreary—
For the plot was void of interest; 'twas the Postal
      Guide, in fact—
There I learnt the true location, distance, size, and
      population
Of each township, town, and village in the radius
      of the Act.

And I learnt that Puckawidgee stands beside the
      Murrumbidgee,
And that Booleroi and Bumble get their letters
      twice a year,
Also that the post inspector, when he visited
      Collector,
Closed the office up instanter, and re-opened Dun-
      galear.

But my languid mood forsook me, when I found
      a name that took me;
Quite by chance I came across it—'Come-by-
      Chance' was what I read;

No location was assigned it, not a thing to help one
    find it,
Just an N which stood for northward, and the rest
    was all unsaid.

I shall leave my home, and forthward wander
    stoutly to the northward
Till I come by chance across it, and I'll straight-
    way settle down;
For there can't be any hurry, nor the slightest
    cause for worry
Where the telegraph don't reach you nor the rail-
    ways run to town.

And one's letters and exchanges come by chance
    across the ranges,
Where a wiry young Australian leads a pack-horse
    once a week,
And the good news grows by keeping, and you're
    spared the pain of weeping
Over bad news when the mailman drops the letters
    in the creek.

But I fear, and more's the pity, that there's really
    no such city,
For there's not a man can find it of the shrewdest
    folk I know;
'Come-by-Chance', be sure it never means a land
    of fierce endeavour—
It is just the careless country where the dreamers
    only go.

·   ·   ·

Though we work and toil and hustle in our life of
    haste and bustle,
All that makes our life worth living comes un-
    striven for and free;

Man may weary and importune, but the fickle
    goddess Fortune
Deals him out his pain or pleasure, careless what
    his worth may be.

All the happy times entrancing, days of sport and
    nights of dancing,
Moonlit rides and stolen kisses, pouting lips and
    loving glance:
When you think of these be certain you have looked
    behind the curtain,
You have had the luck to linger just a while in
    'Come-by-Chance'.

Bulletin, 21 March 1891

JIM CAREW

Born of a thoroughbred English race,
    Well proportioned and closely knit,
Neat, slim figure and handsome face,
    Always ready and always fit,
Hardy and wiry of limb and thew,
That was the ne'er-do-well Jim Carew.

One of the sons of the good old land—
    Many a year since his like was known;
Never a game but he took command,
    Never a sport but he held his own;
Gained at his college a triple blue—
Good as they make them was Jim Carew.

Came to grief—was it card or horse?
    Nobody asked and nobody cared;
Ship him away to the bush of course,
    Ne'er-do-well fellows are easily spared;
Only of women a sorrowing few
Wept at parting from Jim Carew.

Gentleman Jim on the cattle-camp,
    Sitting his horse with an easy grace;
But the reckless living has left its stamp
    In the deep drawn lines of that handsome
        face,
And a harder look in those eyes of blue:
Prompt at a quarrel is Jim Carew.

Billy the Lasher was out for gore—
    Twelve-stone navvy with chest of hair—
When he opened out with a hungry roar
    On a ten-stone man, it was hardly fair;
But his wife was wise if his face she knew
By the time you were done with him, Jim Carew.

Gentleman Jim in the stockmen's hut
    Works with them, toils with them, side by side;
As to his past—well, his lips are shut.
    'Gentleman once,' say his mates with pride;
And the wildest Cornstalk can ne'er outdo
In feats of recklessness Jim Carew.

What should he live for? A dull despair!
    Drink is his master and drags him down,
Water of Lethe that drowns all care.
    Gentleman Jim has a lot to drown,
And he reigns as king with a drunken crew,
Sinking to misery, Jim Carew.

Such is the end of the ne'er-do-well—
    Jimmy the Boozer, all down at heel;
But he straightens up when he's asked to tell
    His name and race, and a flash of steel
Still lightens up in those eyes of blue—
'I am, or—no, I *was*—Jim Carew.'

The Man from Snowy River, 1895

THE SWAGMAN'S REST

We buried old Bob where the bloodwoods wave
   At the foot of the Eaglehawk;
We fashioned a cross on the old man's grave
   For fear that his ghost might walk;
We carved his name on a bloodwood tree
   With the date of his sad decease,
And in place of 'Died from effects of spree'
   We wrote 'May he rest in peace'.

For Bob was known on the Overland,
   A regular old bush wag,
Tramping along in the dust and sand,
   Humping his well-worn swag.
He would camp for days in the river-bed,
   And loiter and 'fish for whales.'
'I'm into the swagman's yard,' he said,
   'And I never shall find the rails'.

But he found the rails on that summer night
   For a better place—or worse,
As we watched by turns in the flickering light
   With an old black gin for nurse.
The breeze came in with the scent of pine,
   The river sounded clear,
When a change came on, and we saw the sign
   That told us the end was near.

He spoke in a cultured voice and low—
   'I fancy they've "sent the route";
I once was an army man, you know,
   Though now I'm a drunken brute;
But bury me out where the bloodwoods wave,
   And, if ever you're fairly stuck,
Just take and shovel me out of the grave
   And, maybe, I'll bring you luck.

'For I've always heard—' here his voice grew weak,
  His strength was wellnigh sped,
He gasped and struggled and tried to speak,
  Then fell in a moment—dead.
Thus ended a wasted life and hard,
  Of energies misapplied—
Old Bob was out of the 'swagman's yard'
  And over the Great Divide.

• • •

The drought came down on the field and flock,
  And never a raindrop fell,
Though the tortured moans of the starving stock
  Might soften a fiend from hell.
And we thought of the hint that the swagman gave
  When he went to the Great Unseen—
We shovelled the skeleton out of the grave
  To see what his hint might mean.

We dug where the cross and the grave posts were,
  We shovelled away the mould,
When sudden a vein of quartz lay bare
  All gleaming with yellow gold.
'Twas a reef with never a fault nor baulk
  That ran from the range's crest,
And the richest mine on the Eaglehawk
  Is known as 'The Swagman's Rest'.

The Man from Snowy River, 1895

THE DAYLIGHT IS DYING

The daylight is dying
  Away in the west,
The wild birds are flying
  In silence to rest;

In leafage and frondage
　　Where shadows are deep,
They pass to its bondage—
　　The kingdom of sleep.

And watched in their sleeping
　　By stars in the height,
They rest in your keeping,
　　O wonderful night.
When night doth her glories
　　Of starshine unfold,
'Tis then that the stories
　　Of bush-land are told.

Unnumbered I hold them
　　In memories bright,
But who could unfold them,
　　Or read them aright?
Beyond all denials
　　The stars in their glories,
The breeze in the myalls,
　　Are part of these stories.

The waving of grasses,
　　The song of the river
That sings as it passes
　　For ever and ever,
The hobble-chains' rattle,
　　The calling of birds,
The lowing of cattle
　　Must blend with the words.

Without these, indeed, you
　　Would find it ere long,
As though I should read you
　　The words of a song

That lamely would linger
  When lacking the rune,
The voice of a singer,
  The lilt of the tune.

But, as one half-hearing
  An old-time refrain,
With memory clearing,
  Recalls it again,
These tales roughly wrought of
  The Bush and its ways,
May call back a thought of
  The wandering days;
And, blending with each
  In the memories that throng
There haply shall reach
  You some echo of song.

The Man from Snowy River, 1895

BY THE GREY GULF-WATER

Far to the Northward there lies a land,
  A wonderful land that the winds blow over,
And none may fathom or understand
  The charm it holds for the restless rover;
A great grey chaos—a land half made,
  Where endless space is and no life stirreth;
There the soul of a man will recoil afraid
  From the sphinx-like visage that Nature weareth.
But old Dame Nature, though scornful, craves
  Her dole of death and her share of slaughter;
Many indeed are the nameless graves
  Where her victims sleep by the Grey Gulf-water.

Slowly and slowly those grey streams glide,
  Drifting along with a languid motion,
Lapping the reed-beds on either side,
  Wending their way to the Northern Ocean.
Grey are the plains where the emus pass
  Silent and slow, with their staid demeanour;
Over the dead men's graves the grass
  Maybe is waving a trifle greener.
Down in the world where men toil and spin
  Dame Nature smiles as man's hand has taught her;
Only the dead men her smiles can win
  In the great lone land by the Grey Gulf-water.

For the strength of man is an insect's strength
  In the face of that mighty plain and river,
And the life of a man is a moment's length
  To the life of the stream that will run for ever.
And so it comes that they take no part
  In small world worries; each hardy rover
Rides like a paladin, light of heart,
  With the plains around and the blue sky over.
And up in the heavens the brown lark sings
  The songs that the strange wild land has taught
    her;
Full of thanksgiving her sweet song rings—
  And I wish I were back in the Grey Gulf-water.

Bulletin, 11 December 1897

SALTBUSH BILL

Now this is the law of the Overland that all in the
    West obey—
A man must cover with travelling sheep a six-mile
    stage a day;

But this is the law which the drovers make, right
    easily understood,
They travel their stage where the grass is bad,
    but they camp where the grass is good;
They camp, and they ravage the squatter's grass
    till never a blade remains,
Then they drift away as the white clouds drift on
    the edge of the saltbush plains;
From camp to camp and from run to run they battle
    it hand to hand
For a blade of grass and the right to pass on the
    track of the Overland.
For this is the law of the Great Stock Routes, 'tis
    written in white and black—
The man that goes with a travelling mob must keep
    to a half-mile track;
And the drovers keep to a half-mile track on the
    runs where the grass is dead,
But they spread their sheep on a well-grassed run
    till they go with a two-mile spread.
So the squatters hurry the drovers on from dawn
    till the fall of night,
And the squatters' dogs and the drovers' dogs get
    mixed in a deadly fight.
Yet the squatters' men, though they hunt the mob,
    are willing the peace to keep,
For the drovers learn how to use their hands when
    they go with the travelling sheep.
But this is the tale of a Jackaroo that came from a
    foreign strand,
And the fight that he fought with Saltbush Bill,
    the King of the Overland.

Now Saltbush Bill was a drover tough as ever the
    country knew,
He had fought his way on the Great Stock Routes
    from the sea to the big Barcoo;

He could tell when he came to a friendly run that
    gave him a chance to spread,
And he knew where the hungry owners were that
    hurried his sheep ahead;
He was drifting down in the Eighty drought with a
    mob that could scarcely creep
(When the kangaroos by the thousand starve, it is
    rough on the travelling sheep),
And he camped one night at the crossing-place on
    the edge of the Wilga run;
'We must manage a feed for them here,' he said,
    'or half of the mob are done!'
So he spread them out when they left the camp
    wherever they liked to go,
Till he grew aware of a Jackaroo with a station-
    hand in tow.
They set to work on the straggling sheep, and with
    many a stockwhip crack
They forced them in where the grass was dead in
    the space of the half-mile track;
And William prayed that the hand of Fate might
    suddenly strike him blue
But he'd get some grass for his starving sheep in
    the teeth of that Jackaroo.
So he turned and he cursed the Jackaroo; he cursed
    him, alive or dead,
From the soles of his great unwieldy feet to the
    crown of his ugly head,
With an extra curse on the moke he rode and the
    cur at his heels that ran,
Till the Jackaroo from his horse got down and went
    for the drover-man;
With the station-hand for his picker-up, though the
    sheep ran loose the while,
They battled it out on the well-grassed plain in the
    regular prize-ring style.

Now, the new chum fought for his honour's sake
    and the pride of the English race,
But the drover fought for his daily bread with a
    smile on his bearded face;
So he shifted ground, and he sparred for wind, and
    he made it a lengthy mill,
And from time to time as his scouts came in they
    whispered to Saltbush Bill—
'We have spread the sheep with a two-mile spread,
    and the grass it is something grand;
You must stick to him, Bill, for another round
    for the pride of the Overland.'
The new chum made it a rushing fight, though never
    a blow got home,
Till the sun rode high in the cloudless sky and
    glared on the brick-red loam,
Till the sheep drew in to the shelter-trees and
    settled them down to rest;
Then the drover said he would fight no more, and
    gave his opponent best.

So the new chum rode to the homestead straight,
    and told them a story grand
Of the desperate fight that he fought that day with
    the King of the Overland;
And the tale went home to the Public Schools of
    the pluck of the English swell—
How the drover fought for his very life, but blood
    in the end must tell.
But the travelling sheep and the Wilga sheep were
    boxed on the Old Man Plain;
'Twas a full week's work ere they drafted out and
    hunted them off again;
A week's good grass in their wretched hides, with
    a curse and a stockwhip crack
They hunted them off on the road once more to
    starve on the half-mile track.

And Saltbush Bill, on the Overland, will many a
   time recite
How the best day's work that he ever did was the
   day that he lost the fight.

Bulletin, 15 December 1894

SALTBUSH BILL'S GAMECOCK

'Twas Saltbush Bill, with his travelling sheep, was
   making his way to town;
He crossed them over the Hard Times Run, and he
   came to the Take 'Em Down;
He counted through at the boundary gate, and
   camped at the drafting yard:
For Stingy Smith, of the Hard Times Run, had
   hunted him rather hard.
He bore no malice to Stingy Smith—'twas simply
   the hand of Fate
That caused his waggon to swerve aside and shatter
   old Stingy's gate;
And being only the hand of Fate, it follows, with-
   out a doubt,
It wasn't the fault of Saltbush Bill that Stingy's
   sheep got out.
So Saltbush Bill, with an easy heart, prepared for
   what might befall,
Commenced his stages on Take 'Em Down, the
   station of Rooster Hall.

'Tis strange how often the men out back will take
   to some curious craft,
Some ruling passion to keep their thoughts away
   from the overdraft;

And Rooster Hall, of the Take 'Em Down, was
    widely known to fame
As breeder of champion fighting cocks—his *forte*
    was the British Game.
The passing stranger within his gates that camped
    with old Rooster Hall
Was forced to talk about fowls all night, or else not
    talk at all.
Though droughts should come, and though sheep
    should die, his fowls were his sole delight;
He left his shed in the flood of work to watch two
    gamecocks fight.
He held in scorn the Australian Game, that long-
    legged child of sin;
In a desperate fight, with the steel-tipped spurs, the
    British Game must win!
The Australian bird was a mongrel bird, with a
    touch of the jungle cock;
The want of breeding must find him out, when
    facing the English stock;
For British breeding, and British pluck, must
    triumph it over all—
And that was the root of the simple creed that
    governed old Rooster Hall.

'Twas Saltbush Bill to the station rode ahead of his
    travelling sheep,
And sent a message to Rooster Hall that wakened
    him out of his sleep—
A crafty message that fetched him out, and hurried
    him as he came—
'A drover has an Australian bird to match with
    your British Game.'
'Twas done, and done in half a trice; a five-pound
    note a side;
Old Rooster Hall, with his champion bird, and the
    drover's bird untried.

'Steel spurs, of course?' said old Rooster Hall;
    'you'll need 'em, without a doubt!'
'You stick the spurs on your bird!' said Bill, 'but
    mine fights best without.'
'Fights best without?' said old Rooster Hall; 'he
    can't fight best unspurred!
You must be crazy!' But Saltbush Bill said, 'Wait
    till you see my bird!'
So Rooster Hall to his fowl-yard went, and quickly
    back he came,
Bearing a clipt and a shaven cock, the pride of his
    English Game;
With an eye as fierce as an eaglehawk, and a crow
    like a trumpet call,
He strutted about on the garden walk, and cackled
    at Rooster Hall.
Then Rooster Hall sent off a boy with word to his
    cronies two,
McCrae (the boss of the Black Police) and Father
    Donahoo.
Full many a cockfight old McCrae had held in his
    empty Court,
With Father D. as the picker-up—a regular all-round
    Sport!
They got the message of Rooster Hall, and down to
    his run they came,
Prepared to scoff at the drover's bird, and to bet on
    the English Game;
They hied them off to the drover's camp, while Salt-
    bush rode before—
Old Rooster Hall was a blithesome man, when he
    thought of the treat in store.
They reached the camp, where the drover's cook,
    with countenance all serene,
Was boiling beef in an iron pot, but never a fowl
    was seen.

'Take off the beef from the fire,' said Bill, 'and
    wait till you see the fight;
There's something fresh for the bill-of-fare—there's
    game-fowl stew to-night!
For Mister Hall has a fighting cock, all feathered
    and clipped and spurred;
And he's fetched him here, for a bit of sport, to
    fight our Australian bird.
I've made a match that our pet will win, though
    he's hardly a fighting cock,
But he's game enough, and it's many a mile that
    he's tramped with the travelling stock.'
The cook he banged on a saucepan lid; and, soon as
    the sound was heard,
Under the dray, in the shadow hid, a something
    moved and stirred:
A great tame emu strutted out. Said Saltbush,
    'Here's our bird!'
But Rooster Hall, and his cronies two, drove home
    without a word.

The passing stranger within his gates that camps
    with old Rooster Hall
Must talk about something else than fowls, if he
    wishes to talk at all.
For the record lies in the local Court, and filed in
    its deepest vault,
That Peter Hall, of the Take 'Em Down, was tried
    for a fierce assault
On a stranger man, who, in all good faith, and
    prompted by what he heard,
Had asked old Hall if a British Game could beat an
    Australian bird;
And old McCrae, who was on the Bench, as soon
    as the case was tried,
Remarked, 'Discharged with a clean discharge—the
    assault was justified!'

Rio Grande's Last Race, 1902

SALTBUSH BILL'S SECOND FIGHT

The news came down on the Castlereagh, and went
    to the world at large,
That twenty thousand travelling sheep, with Salt-
    bush Bill in charge,
Were drifting down from a dried-out run to ravage
    the Castlereagh;
And the squatters swore when they heard the news,
    and wished they were well away:
For the name and the fame of Saltbush Bill were
    over the country-side,
For the wonderful way that he fed his sheep, and
    the dodges and tricks he tried.

He would lose his way on a Main Stock Route, and
    stray to the squatters' grass;
He would come to a run with the boss away, and
    swear he had leave to pass;
And back of all and behind it all, as well the
    squatters knew,
If he had to fight, he would fight all day, so long as
    his sheep got through:
But this is the story of Stingy Smith, the owner of
    Hard Times Hill,
And the way that he chanced on a fighting man to
    reckon with Saltbush Bill.

       •   •   •

'Twas Stingy Smith on his stockyard sat, and prayed
    for an early Spring,
When he started at sight of a clean-shaved tramp,
    who walked with a jaunty swing;
For a clean-shaved tramp with a jaunty walk
    a-swinging along the track
Is as rare a thing as a feathered frog on the desolate
    roads out back.

So the tramp he made for the traveller's hut, to ask
    could he camp the night;
But Stingy Smith had a bright idea, and called to
    him, 'Can you fight?'

'Why, what's the game?' said the clean-shaved
    tramp, as he looked at him up and down;
'If you want a battle, get off that fence, and I'll kill
    you for half-a-crown!
But, Boss, you'd better not fight with me—it
    wouldn't be fair nor right;
I'm Stiffener Joe, from the Rocks Brigade, and I
    killed a man in a fight:
I served two years for it, fair and square, and now
    I'm a-trampin' back,
To look for a peaceful quiet life away on the outside
    track.'

'Oh, it's not myself, but a drover chap,' said Stingy
    Smith with glee;
'A bullying fellow called Saltbush Bill, and you are
    the man for me.
He's on the road with his hungry sheep, and he's
    certain to raise a row,
For he's bullied the whole of the Castlereagh till he's
    got them under cow—
Just pick a quarrel and raise a fight, and leather
    him good and hard,
And I'll take good care that his wretched sheep
    don't wander a half a yard.
It's a five-pound job if you belt him well—do any-
    thing short of kill,
For there isn't a beak on the Castlereagh will fine
    you for Saltbush Bill.'

'I'll take the job,' said the fighting man; 'and, hot
    as this cove appears,
He'll stand no chance with a bloke like me, what's
    lived on the game for years;
For he's maybe learnt in a boxing school, and
    sparred for a round or so,
But I've fought all hands in a ten-foot ring each
    night in a travelling show;
They earned a pound if they stayed three rounds,
    and they tried for it every night
In a ten-foot ring! Oh, that's the game that teaches
    a bloke to fight,
For they'd rush and clinch—it was Dublin Rules,
    and we drew no colour line;
And they all tried hard for to earn the pound, but
    they got no pound of mine:
If I saw no chance in the opening round I'd slog at
    their wind, and wait
Till an opening came—and it *always* came—and I
    settled 'em, sure as fate;
Left on the ribs and right on the jaw—and, when
    the chance comes, make sure!
And it's there a professional bloke like me gets
    home on an amateur:
For it's my experience every day, and I make no
    doubt it's yours,
That a third-class pro is an over-match for the best
    of the amateurs—'
'Oh, take your swag to the travellers' hut,' said
    Smith, 'for you waste your breath;
You've a first-class chance, if you lose the fight, of
    talking your man to death.
I'll tell the cook you're to have your grub, and see
    that you eat your fill,
And come to the scratch all fit and well to leather
    this Saltbush Bill.'

      •   •   •

'Twas Saltbush Bill, and his travelling sheep were
    wending their weary way
On the Main Stock Route, through the Hard Times
    Run, on their six-mile stage a day;
And he strayed a mile from the Main Stock Route,
    and started to feed along,
And when Stingy Smith came up Bill said that the
    Route was surveyed wrong;
And he tried to prove that the sheep had rushed and
    strayed from their camp at night,
But the fighting man he kicked Bill's dog, and of
    course that meant a fight.

So they sparred and fought, and they shifted ground,
    and never a sound was heard
But the thudding fists on their brawny ribs, and the
    seconds' muttered word,
Till the fighting man shot home his left on the ribs
    with a mighty clout,
And his right flashed up with a half-arm blow—and
    Saltbush Bill 'went out'.
He fell face down, and towards the blow; and their
    hearts with fear were filled,
For he lay as still as a fallen tree, and they thought
    that he must be killed.

So Stingy Smith and the fighting man, they lifted
    him from the ground,
And sent back home for a brandy-flask, and they
    slowly fetched him round;
But his head was bad, and his jaw was hurt—in fact,
    he could scarcely speak—
So they let him spell till he got his wits; and he
    camped on the run a week,

While the travelling sheep went here and there,
    wherever they liked to stray,
Till Saltbush Bill was fit once more for the track
    to the Castlereagh.

• • •

Then Stingy Smith he wrote a note, and gave to the
    fighting man:
'Twas writ to the boss of the neighbouring run, and
    thus the missive ran:
'The man with this is a fighting man, one Stiffener
    Joe by name;
He came near murdering Saltbush Bill, and I found
    it a costly game:
But it's worth your while to employ the chap, for
    there isn't the slightest doubt
You'll have no trouble from Saltbush Bill while this
    man hangs about.'

But an answer came by the next week's mail, with
    news that might well appal:
'The man you sent with a note is not a fighting
    man at all!
He has shaved his beard, and has cut his hair, but I
    spotted him at a look;
He is Tom Devine, who has worked for years for
    Saltbush Bill as cook.
Bill coached him up in the fighting yarn, and taught
    him the tale by rote,
And they shammed to fight, and they got your grass,
    and divided your five-pound note.
'Twas a clean take-in; and you'll find it wise—'twill
    save you a lot of pelf—
When next you're hiring a fighting man, just fight
    him a round yourself.'

• • •

And the teamsters out on the Castlereagh, when
    they meet with a week of rain,
And the waggon sinks to its axle-tree, deep down in
    the black-soil plain,
When the bullocks wade in a sea of mud, and strain
    at the load of wool,
And the cattle-dogs at the bullocks' heels are biting
    to make them pull,
When the off-side driver flays the team, and curses
    them while he flogs,
And the air is thick with the language used, and the
    clamour of men and dogs—
The teamsters say, as they pause to rest and
    moisten each hairy throat,
They wish they could swear like Stingy Smith when
    he read that neighbour's note.

Rio Grande's Last Race, 1902

SALTBUSH BILL, J.P.

Beyond the land where Leichhardt went,
    Beyond Sturt's Western track,
The rolling tide of change has sent
    Some strange J.P.'s out back.

And Saltbush Bill, grown old and grey,
    And worn for want of sleep,
Received the news in camp one day
    Behind the travelling sheep.

That Edward Rex, confiding in
    His known integrity,
By hand and seal on parchment skin
    Had made him a J.P.

He read the news with eager face
    But found no word of pay.
'I'd like to see my sister's place
    And kids on Christmas Day.

'I'd like to see green grass again,
    And watch clear water run,
Away from this unholy plain,
    And flies, and dust, and sun.'

At last one little clause he found
    That might some hope inspire,
'A magistrate may charge a pound
    For inquest on a fire.'

A big blacks' camp was built close by,
    And Saltbush Bill, says he,
'I think that camp might well supply
    A job for a J.P.'

That night, by strange coincidence,
    A most disastrous fire
Destroyed the country residence
    Of Jacky Jack, Esquire.

'Twas mostly leaves, and bark, and dirt;
    The party most concerned
Appeared to think it wouldn't hurt
    If forty such were burned.

Quite otherwise thought Saltbush Bill,
    Who watched the leaping flame.
'The home is small,' said he, 'but still
    The principle's the same.

'Midst palaces though you should roam,
    Or follow pleasure's tracks,
You'll find,' he said, 'no place like home—
    At least like Jacky Jack's.

'Tell every man in camp "Come quick,"
  Tell every black Maria
I give tobacco, half a stick—
  Hold inquest long-a fire.'

Each juryman received a name
  Well suited to a Court.
'Long Jack' and 'Stumpy Bill' became
  'John Long' and 'William Short'.

While such as 'Tarpot', 'Bullock Dray',
  And 'Tommy Wait-a-While',
Became, for ever and a day,
  'Scott', 'Dickens', and 'Carlyle'.

And twelve good sable men and true
  Were soon engaged upon
The conflagration that o'erthrew
  The home of John A. John.

Their verdict, 'Burnt by act of Fate',
  They scarcely had returned
When, just behind the magistrate,
  Another humpy burned!

The jury sat again and drew
  Another stick of plug.
Said Saltbush Bill, 'It's up to you
  Put some one long-a Jug'.

'I'll camp the sheep', he said, 'and sift
  The evidence about'.
For quite a week he couldn't shift,
  The way the fires broke out.

The jury thought the whole concern
  As good as any play.
They used to 'take him oath' and earn
  Three sticks of plug a day.

At last the tribe lay down to sleep
  Homeless, beneath a tree;
And onward with his travelling sheep
  Went Saltbush Bill, J.P.

The sheep delivered, safe and sound,
  His horse to town he turned,
And drew some five-and-twenty pound
  For fees that he had earned.

And where Monaro's ranges hide
  Their little farms away—
His sister's children by his side—
  He spent his Christmas Day.

The next J.P. that went out back
  Was shocked, or pained, or both,
At hearing every pagan black
  Repeat the juror's oath.

No matter though he turned and fled
  They followed faster still;
'You make it inkwich, boss', they said,
  'All same like Saltbush Bill.'

They even said they'd let him see
  The fires originate.
When he refused they said that he
  Was 'No good magistrate'.

And out beyond Sturt's Western track,
  And Leichhardt's farthest tree,
They wait till fate shall send them back
  Their Saltbush Bill, J.P.

Saltbush Bill, J.P., 1917

HAY AND HELL AND BOOLIGAL

'You come and see me, boys,' he said;
You'll find a welcome and a bed
  And whisky and time you call;
Although our township hasn't got
The name of quite a lively spot—
  You see, I live in Booligal.

'And people have an awful down
Upon the district and the town—
  Which worse than hell itself they call;
In fact, the saying far and wide
Along the Riverina side
  Is 'Hay and Hell and Booligal'.

'No doubt it suits 'em very well
To say it's worse than Hay or Hell,
  But don't you heed their talk at all;
Of course, there's heat—no one denies—
And sand and dust and stacks of flies,
  And rabbits, too, at Booligal.

'But such a pleasant, quiet place—
You never see a stranger's face;
  They hardly ever care to call;
The drovers mostly pass it by—
They reckon that they'd rather die
  Than spend the night in Booligal.

'The big mosquitoes frighten some—
You'll lie awake to hear 'em hum—
  And snakes about the township crawl;
But shearers, when they get their cheque,
They never come along and wreck
  The blessed town of Booligal.

Bulletin, 25 April 1896

BRUMBY'S RUN

*Brumby is the Aboriginal word for a wild horse.
At a recent trial a New South Wales Supreme
Court Judge, hearing of Brumby horses, asked:
'Who is Brumby, and where is his Run?'*

It lies beyond the Western Pines
   Beneath the sinking sun,
And not a survey mark defines
   The bounds of 'Brumby's Run'.

On odds and ends of mountain land,
   On tracks of range and rock
Where no one else can make a stand
   Old Brumby rears his stock.

A wild, unhandled lot they are
   Of every shape and breed.
They venture out 'neath moon and star
   Along the flats to feed;

But, when the dawn makes pink the sky
   And steals along the plain,
The Brumby horses turn and fly
   Back to the hills again.

The traveller by the mountain-track
   May hear their hoof-beats pass,
And catch a glimpse of brown and black
   Dim shadows on the grass.

The eager stock-horse pricks his ears,
   And lifts his head on high
In wild excitement, when he hears
   The Brumby mob go by.

Old Brumby asks no price or fee
   O'er all his wide domains:
The man who yards his stock is free
   To keep them for his pains.

So, off to scour the mountain side
   With eager eyes aglow,
To strongholds where the wild mobs hide
   The gully-rakers go.

A rush of horses through the trees,
   A red shirt making play;
A sound of stockwhips on the breeze,
   They vanish far away!

     •   •   •

Ah, me! before our day is done
   We long with bitter pain
To ride once more on Brumby's Run
   And yard his mob again.

Bulletin, 21 December 1895

WALTZING MATILDA

(Carrying a Swag.)

Oh! there once was a swagman camped in a
   Billabong,
  Under the shade of a Coolabah tree;
And he sang as he looked at his old billy boiling,
  'Who'll come a-waltzing Matilda with me?'

   Who'll come a-waltzing Matilda, my darling,
    Who'll come a-waltzing Matilda with me?
   Waltzing Matilda and leading a water-bag—
    Who'll come a-waltzing Matilda with me?

Down came a jumbuck to drink at the water-hole,
  Up jumped the swagman and grabbed him in glee;
And he sang as he stowed him away in his tucker-
      bag,
  'You'll come a-waltzing Matilda with me!'

Down came the Squatter a-riding his thoroughbred;
  Down came Policemen—one, two and three.
'Whose is the jumbuck you've got in the tucker-
      bag?
  You'll come a-waltzing Matilda with me.'

But the swagman, he up and he jumped in the water-
      hole,
  Drowning himself by the Coolabah tree;
And his ghost may be heard as it sings in the Billa-
      bong
  'Who'll come a-waltzing Matilda with me?'

First published *c.* 1903 by Inglis &
Co. with sheet music. This version
published in 1917 in *Saltbush Bill,
J.P.*

The Sporting Life

. . . I'll never back horses at seven to four . . .

The Camden Team: H.L. Mackellar, V.G. Maddox,
A.B. Paterson, Dr Bell

When Banjo Paterson wrote his reminiscences in 1939 there were still more than 1 700 000 horses in Australia. His lifetime spanned the era of the horse in this country. There were work horses, stock and draught horses; the 'Walers' bred for export for the Indian army; and, of course, the racehorses and the polo ponies, of varying breeding—Paterson wrote about them all. The balladist, with some reason, described himself as 'horse-mad'. From the first race-meeting he attended at Binalong, aged eight, until the onset of his last illness, Banjo Paterson was at the track. His sharp ear and shrewd eye observed not only the horses but the human medley. He was not detached, being prepared to see the exploitation of the young jockey, his older peers or the battling steeplechase riders, or to complain about crooked stewards. Paterson may not have died wealthy, but it's a fortunate man who can make his living doing what he likes best.

Paterson outlived the age of statues. Lawson, safely dead, was given one in the Sydney Domain, where, ironically, he had slept out in earlier years. Adam Lindsay Gordon, their predecessor, got one in Melbourne, seated in a chair, because not enough money was raised to fulfil the original plan to show him mounted.

If a place had to be found for a statue of Banjo Paterson it should not be in the Snowy Mountains, but rather at Randwick racecourse, somewhere near the old members' stand, standing with those outsized binoculars around his neck waiting for the next race. The Banjo would have liked that.

'WHEN I WENT TO THE BAR'
A RACING RHYME

(with apologies to W.S. Gilbert)

When I went to the bar as a very young man,
  Said I to the girl, said I,
I've hit on a new and original plan
  To do without work, said I.
So if you'll be pleasant and listen, my dear,
And chuck me a simper and lend me your ear,
I'll tell you the tale while you draw me a beer.
  Said I to the girl, said I.

I'll never back horses at seven to four,
  Said I to the girl, said I.
Who start in a field that is over a score,
  Said I to the girl, said I.
There's always a chance of them missing a place
Through getting a bump or the luck of the race,
And laying odds on is 'the end of the case',
  Said I to the girl, said I.

I'll never get 'in' while the stable is 'out',
  Said I to the girl, said I.
I'm looking for trouble without any doubt,
  Said I to the girl, said I.
For getting in early and trusting your luck,
Perhaps is a symptom of wonderful pluck.
But what ho! when it finishes back in the
    ruck.
  Said I to the girl, said I.

Then backing outsiders is always a 'nark',
  Said I to the girl, said I.
Because of some gallop they did in the dark,
  Said I to the girl, said I.

I'm sure to go broke if I heed the romance
Of jokers who haven't a seat in their pants,
And lumber me on to some any-price chance,
    Said I to the girl, said I.

I'm satisfied this is a payable lurk,
    Said I to the girl, said I.
To follow a trainer who's good at his work,
    Said I to the girl, said I.
When he goes in the ring and I stand on the
        brink,
And he puts in the poultice and gives me a wink,
I'll never ask questions, or listen, or think,
    Said I to the girl, said I.

So now I've discovered the key of the game,
    Said I to the girl, said I.
We'll drink to success in a pint of the same,
    Said I to the girl, said I.
For following jockeys may do for a muff,
And following gallops—I've tried enough—
The road to success is to 'follow the stuff',
    Said I to the girl, said I.

U.K. Lely
(*'Poultice' is slang for a large bet*)

Sydney Sportsman, 31 August 1921

A DREAM OF THE MELBOURNE CUP

(1886)

Bring me a quart of colonial beer
And some doughy damper to make good cheer,
    I must make a heavy dinner;

Heavily dine and heavily sup,
Of indigestible things fill up,
Next month they run the Melbourne Cup,
   And I have to dream the winner.

Stoke it in, boys! the half-cooked ham,
The rich ragout and the charming cham.,
   I've got to mix my liquor;
Give me a gander's gaunt hind leg,
Hard and tough as a wooden peg,
And I'll keep it down with a hard-boiled egg,
   'Twill make me dream the quicker.

Now that I'm full of fearful feed,
Oh, but I'll dream of a winner indeed
   In my restless, troubled slumber;
While the night-mares race through my heated brain
And their devil-riders spur amain,
The tip for the Cup will reward my pain,
   And I'll spot the winning number.

      •   •   •

Thousands and thousands and thousands more,
Like sands on the white Pacific shore,
   The crowding people cluster;
For evermore is the story old,
While races are bought and backers are sold,
Drawn by the greed of the gain of gold,
   In their thousands still they muster.

And the bookies' cries grow fierce and hot,
'I'll lay the Cup! The double, if not!'
   'Five monkeys, Little John, sir!'
'Here's fives bar one, I lay, I lay!'
And so they shout through the livelong day,
And stick to the game that is sure to pay,
   While fools put money on, sir!

And now in my dream I seem to go
And bet with a 'book' that I seem to know—
    A Hebrew money-lender;
A million to five is the price I get—
Not bad! but before I book the bet
The horse's name I clean forget,
    Its number and even gender.

Now for the start, and here they come,
And the hoof-strokes roar like a mighty drum
    Beat by a hand unsteady;
They come like a rushing, roaring flood,
Hurrah for the speed of the Chester blood;
For Acme is making the pace so good
    There are some of 'em done already.

But round the back she begins to tire,
And a mighty shout goes up 'Crossfire!'
    The magpie jacket's leading;
And Crossfire challenges, fierce and bold,
And the lead she'll have and the lead she'll hold,
But at length gives way to the black and gold,
    Which right to the front is speeding.

Carry them on and keep it up—
A flying race is the Melbourne Cup,
    You must race and stay to win it;
And old Commotion, Victoria's pride,
Now takes the lead with his raking stride,
And a mighty roar goes far and wide—
    'There's only Commotion in it!'

But one draws out from the beaten ruck
And up on the rails by a piece of luck
    He comes in a style that's clever;
'It's Trident! Trident! Hurrah for Hales!'
'Go at 'em now while their courage fails;'

'Trident! Trident! for New South Wales!'
  'The blue and white for ever!'

Under the whip! with the ears flat back,
Under the whip! though the sinews crack,
  No sign of the base white feather;
Stick to it now for your breeding's sake,
Stick to it now though your hearts should break,
While the yells and roars make the grand-stand
      shake,
  They come down the straight together.

Trident slowly forges ahead,
The fierce whips cut and the spurs are red,
  The pace is undiminished;
Now for the Panics that never fail!
But many a backer's face grows pale
As old Commotion swings his tail
  And swerves—and the Cup is finished.

·　　·　　·

And now in my dream it all comes back:
I bet my coin on the Sydney crack,
  A million I've won, no question!
'Give me my money, you hook-nosed hog!
Give me my money, bookmaking dog!'
But he disappeared in a kind of fog,
  And I woke with 'the indigestion'.

Bulletin, 30 October 1886

OLD PARDON, THE SON OF REPRIEVE

  You never heard tell of the story?
    Well, now, I can hardly believe!

Never heard of the honour and glory
    Of Pardon, the son of Reprieve?
But maybe you're only a Johnnie
    And don't know a horse from a hoe?
Well, well, don't get angry, my sonny,
    But, really, a young un should know.

They bred him out back on the 'Never',
    His mother was Mameluke breed.
To the front—and then stay there—was ever
    The root of the Mameluke creed.
He seemed to inherit their wiry
    Strong frames—and their pluck to receive—
As hard as a flint and as fiery
    Was Pardon, the son of Reprieve.

We ran him at many a meeting
    At crossing and gully and town,
And nothing could give him a beating—
    At least when our money was down.
For weight wouldn't stop him, nor distance,
    Nor odds, though the others were fast;
He'd race with a dogged persistence,
    And wear them all down at the last.

At the Turon the Yattendon filly
    Led by lengths at the mile-and-a-half,
And we all began to look silly,
    While her crowd were starting to laugh;
But the old horse came faster and faster,
    His pluck told its tale, and his strength,
He gained on her, caught her, and passed her,
    And won it, hands-down, by a length.

And then we swooped down on Menindie
    To run for the President's Cup;
Oh! that's a sweet township—a shindy
    To them is board, lodging, and sup.

Eye-openers they are, and their system
  Is never to suffer defeat;
It's 'win, tie, or wrangle'—to best 'em
  You must lose 'em, or else it's 'dead heat'.

We strolled down the township and found 'em
  At drinking and gaming and play;
If sorrows they had, why they drowned 'em,
  And betting was soon under way.
Their horses were good uns and fit uns,
  There was plenty of cash in the town;
They backed their own horses like Britons,
  And, Lord! how *we* rattled it down!

With gladness we thought of the morrow,
  We counted our wagers with glee,
A simile homely to borrow—
  'There was plenty of milk in our tea.'
You see we were green; and we never
  Had even a thought of foul play,
Though we well might have known that the clever
  Division would 'put us away'.

Experience *docet*, they tell us,
  At least so I've frequently heard;
But, 'dosing' or 'stuffing', those fellows
  Were up to each move on the board:
They got to his stall—it is sinful
  To think what such villains will do—
And they gave him a regular skinful
  Of barley—green barley—to chew.

He munched it all night, and we found him
  Next morning as full as a hog—
The girths wouldn't nearly meet round him;
  He looked like an overfed frog.

We saw we were done like a dinner—
  The odds were a thousand to one
Against Pardon turning up winner,
  'Twas cruel to ask him to run.

We got to the course with our troubles,
  A crestfallen couple were we;
And we heard the 'books' calling the doubles—
  A roar like the surf of the sea;
And over the tumult and louder
  Rang 'Any price Pardon, I lay!'
Says Jimmy, 'The Children of Judah
  Are out on the warpath to-day.'

Three miles in three heats:—Ah, my sonny,
  The horses in those days were stout,
They had to run well to win money;
  I don't see such horses about.
Your six-furlong vermin that scamper
  Half-a-mile with their feather-weight up,
They wouldn't earn much of their damper
  In a race like the President's Cup.

The first heat was soon set a-going;
  The Dancer went off to the front;
The Don on his quarters was showing,
  With Pardon right out of the hunt.
He rolled and he weltered and wallowed—
  You'd kick your hat faster, I'll bet;
They finished all bunched, and he followed
  All lathered and dripping with sweat.

But troubles came thicker upon us,
  For while we were rubbing him dry
The stewards came over to warn us:
  'We hear you are running a bye!

If Pardon don't spiel like tarnation
  And win the next heat—if he can—
He'll earn a disqualification;
    Just think over *that* now, my man!'

Our money all gone and our credit,
  Our horse couldn't gallop a yard;
And then people thought that *we* did it!
  It really was terribly hard.
We were objects of mirth and derision
  To folk in the lawn and the stand,
And the yells of the clever division
  Of 'Any price Pardon!' were grand.

We still had a chance for the money,
  Two heats still remained to be run;
If both fell to us—why, my sonny,
  The clever division were done.
And Pardon was better, we reckoned,
  His sickness was passing away,
So he went to the post for the second
  And principal heat of the day.

They're off and away with a rattle,
  Like dogs from the leashes let slip,
And right at the back of the battle
  He followed them under the whip.
They gained ten good lengths on him quickly
  He dropped right away from the pack;
I tell you it made me feel sickly
  To see the blue jacket fall back.

Our very last hope had departed—
  We thought the old fellow was done,
When all of a sudden he started
  To go like a shot from a gun.

His chances seemed slight to embolden
  Our hearts; but, with teeth firmly set,
We thought, 'Now or never! The old un
  May reckon with some of 'em yet.'

Then loud rose the war-cry for Pardon;
  He swept like the wind down the dip,
And over the rise by the garden
  The jockey was done with the whip.
The field were at sixes and sevens—
  The pace at the first had been fast—
And hope seemed to drop from the heavens,
  For Pardon was coming at last.

And how he did come! It was splendid;
  He gained on them yards every bound,
Stretching out like a greyhound extended,
  His girth laid right down on the ground.
A shimmer of silk in the cedars
  As into the running they wheeled,
And out flashed the whips on the leaders,
  For Pardon had collared the field.

Then right through the ruck he came sailing—
  I knew that the battle was won—
The son of Haphazard was failing,
  The Yattendon filly was done;
He cut down The Don and The Dancer,
  He raced clean away from the mare—
He's in front! Catch him now if you can, sir!
  And up went my hat in the air!

Then loud from the lawn and the garden
  Rose offers of 'Ten to one *on*!'
'Who'll bet on the field? I back Pardon!'
  No use; all the money was gone.

He came for the third heat light-hearted,
  A-jumping and dancing about;
The others were done ere they started
  Crestfallen, and tired, and worn out.

He won it, and ran it much faster
  Than even the first, I believe;
Oh, he was the daddy, the master,
  Was Pardon, the son of Reprieve.
He showed 'em the method to travel—
  The boy sat still as a stone—
They never could see him for gravel;
  He came in hard-held, and alone.

But he's old—and his eyes are grown hollow;
  Like me, with my thatch of the snow;
When he dies, then I hope I may follow,
  And go where the racehorses go.
I don't want no harping nor singing—
  Such things with my style don't agree;
Where the hoofs of the horses are ringing
  There's music sufficient for me.

And surely the thoroughbred horses
  Will rise up again and begin
Fresh races on faraway courses,
  And p'raps they might let me slip in.
It would look rather well the race-card on
  'Mongst cherubs and seraphs and things,
'Angel Harrison's black gelding Pardon,
  Blue halo, white body and wings'.

And if they have racing hereafter,
  (And who is to say they will not?)
When the cheers and the shouting and laughter
  Proclaim that the battle grows hot;

As they come down the racecourse a-steering,
　　He'll rust to the front, I believe;
And you'll hear the great multitude cheering
　　For Pardon, the son of Reprieve.

Bulletin, 22 December 1888

THE GEEBUNG POLO CLUB

It was somewhere up the country, in a land of rock
　　and scrub,
That they formed an institution called the Geebung
　　Polo Club.
They were long and wiry natives from the rugged
　　mountainside,
And the horse was never saddled that the Geebungs
　　couldn't ride;
But their style of playing polo was irregular and
　　rash—
They had mighty little science, but a mighty lot
　　of dash:
And they played on mountain ponies that were
　　muscular and strong,
Though their coats were quite unpolished, and their
　　manes and tails were long.
And they used to train those ponies wheeling cattle
　　in the scrub:
They were demons, were the members of the Gee-
　　bung Polo Club.

It was somewhere down the country, in a city's
　　smoke and steam,
That a polo club existed, called 'The Cuff and
　　Collar Team'.

As a social institution 'twas a marvellous success,
For the members were distinguished by exclusive-
     ness and dress.
They had natty little ponies that were nice, and
     smooth, and sleek,
For their cultivated owners only rode 'em once a
     week.
So they started up the country in pursuit of sport
     and fame,
For they meant to show the Geebungs how they
     ought to play the game;
And they took their valets with them—just to give
     their boots a rub
Ere they started operations on the Geebung Polo
     Club.

Now my readers can imagine how the contest ebbed
     and flowed,
When the Geebung boys got going it was time to
     clear the road;
And the game was so terrific that ere half the time
     was gone
A spectator's leg was broken—just from merely
     looking on.
For they waddied one another till the plain was
     strewn with dead,
While the score was kept so even that they neither
     got ahead.
And the Cuff and Collar Captain, when he tumbled
     off to die
Was the last surviving player—so the game was
     called a tie.

Then the Captain of the Geebungs raised him slowly
     from the ground,
Though his wounds were mostly mortal, yet he
     fiercely gazed around;

There was no one to oppose him—all the rest were
  in a trance,
So he scrambled on his pony for his last expiring
  chance,
For he meant to make an effort to get victory to
  his side;
So he struck at goal—and missed it—then he
  tumbled off and died.

•   •   •

By the old Campaspe River, where the breezes
  shake the grass,
There's a row of little gravestones that the stock-
  men never pass,
For they bear a rude inscription saying, 'Stranger,
  drop a tear,
For the Cuff and Collar players and the Geebung
  boys lie here.'
And on misty moonlit evenings, while the dingoes
  howl around,
You can see their shadows flitting down that
  phantom polo ground;
You can hear the loud collisions as the flying players
  meet,
And the rattle of the mallets, and the rush of ponies'
  feet,
Till the terrified spectator rides like blazes to the
  pub—
He's been haunted by the spectres of the Geebung
  Polo Club.

The Antipodean, 1893

THE AMATEUR RIDER

Him going to ride for us! *Him*—with the pants and
  the eyeglass and all.
Amateur! don't he just look it—it's twenty to one
  on a fall.

Boss must be gone off his head to be sending our
    steeplechase crack
Out over fences like these with an object like that
    on his back.

Ride! Don't tell *me* he can ride. With his pants
    just as loose as balloons,
How can he sit on a horse? and his spurs like a
    pair of harpoons;
Ought to be under the Dog Act, he ought, and be
    kept off the course.
Fall! why, he'd fall off a cart, let alone off a steeple-
    chase horse.

      •   •   •

Yessir! the 'orse is all ready—I wish you'd have
    rode him before;
Nothing like knowing your 'orse, sir, and this chap's
    a terror to bore;
Battleaxe always could pull, and he rushes his
    fences like fun—
Stands off his jump twenty feet, and then springs
    like a shot from a gun.

Oh, he can jump 'em all right, sir, you make no
    mistake, 'e's a toff—
Clouts 'em in earnest, too, sometimes; you mind
    that he don't clout you off—
Don't seem to mind how he hits 'em, his shins is as
    hard as a nail,
Sometimes you'll see the fence shake and the
    splinters fly up from the rail.

All you can do is to hold him and just let him jump
    as he likes,
Give him his head at the fences, and hang on like
    death if he strikes;

Don't let him run himself out—you can lie third or
    fourth in the race—
Until you clear the stone wall, and from that you
    can put on the pace.

Fell at that wall once, he did, and it gave him a
    regular spread,
Ever since that time he flies it—he'll stop if you pull
    at his head,
Just let him race—you can trust him—he'll take
    first-class care he don't fall,
And I think that's the lot—but remember, he must
    have his head at the wall.

       •   •   •

Well, he's down safe as far as the start, and he
    seems to sit on pretty neat,
Only his baggified breeches would ruinate anyone's
    seat—
They're away—here they come—the first fence, and
    he's head over heels for a crown!
Good for the new chum, he's over, and two of the
    others are down!

Now for the treble, my hearty—By Jove, he can
    ride, after all;
Whoop, that's your sort—let him fly them! He
    hasn't much fear of a fall.
Who in the world would have thought it? And
    aren't they just going a pace?
Little Recruit in the lead there will make it a stoutly
    run race.

Lord! but they're racing in earnest—and down goes
    Recruit on his head,
Rolling clean over his boy—it's a miracle if he ain't
    dead.

Battleaxe, Battleaxe, yet! By the Lord, he's got
  most of 'em beat—
Ho! did you see how he struck, and the swell never
  moved in his seat?

Second time round, and, by Jingo! he's holding his
  lead of 'em well;
Hark to him clouting the timber! It don't seem to
  trouble the swell.
Now for the wall—let him rush it. A thirty-foot
  leap, I declare—
Never a shift in his seat, and he's racing for home
  like a hare.

What's that chasing him—Rataplan—regular demon
  to stay!
Sit down and ride for your life now! Oh, good, that's
  the style—come away!
Rataplan's certain to beat you, unless you can give
  him the slip;
Sit down and rub in the whalebone now—give him
  the spurs and the whip!

Battleaxe, Battleaxe, yet—and it's Battleaxe wins for
  a crown;
Look at him rushing the fences, he wants to bring
  t'other chap down.
Rataplan never will catch him if only he keeps on
  his pins;
Now! the last fence! and he's over it! Battleaxe,
  Battleaxe wins!

• • •

Well, sir, you rode him just perfect—I knew from
  the first you could ride.
Some of the chaps said you couldn't, an' I says just
  like this a' one side:

Mark me, I says, that's a tradesman—the saddle
    is where he was bred.
Weight! you're all right, sir, and thank you; and
    them was the words that I said.

Bulletin, 15 December 1894

ONLY A JOCKEY

*'Richard Bennison, a jockey, aged fourteen, while riding
William Tell in his training, was thrown and killed. The
horse is luckily uninjured.'*—Melbourne Wire

Out in the grey cheerless chill of the morning light,
    Out on the track where the night shades still lurk,
Ere the first gleam of the sungod's returning light
    Round come the racehorses early at work.

Reefing and pulling and racing so readily,
    Close sit the jockey-boys holding them hard,
'Steady the stallion there—canter him steadily,
    Don't let him gallop so much as a yard.'

Fiercely he fights while the others run wide of him,
    Reefs at the bit that would hold him in thrall,
Plunges and bucks till the boy that's astride of him
    Goes to the ground with a terrible fall.

'Stop him there! Block him there! Drive him in
        carefully,
    Lead him about till he's quiet and cool.
Sound as a bell! though he's blown himself
        fearfully,
    Now let us pick up this poor little fool.

'Stunned? Oh, by Jove, I'm afraid it's a case with
    him,
  Ride for the doctor! keep bathing his head!
Send for a cart to go down to our place with him'—
  No use! One long sigh and the little chap's dead.

Only a jockey-boy! foul-mouthed and bad you see,
  Ignorant, heathenish, gone to his rest.
Parson or Presbyter, Pharisee, Sadducee,
  What did you do for him?—bad was the best.

Negroes and foreigners, all have a claim on you;
  Yearly you send your well-advertised hoard,
But the poor jockey-boy—shame on you, shame on
    you,
  'Feed ye my little ones'—What said the Lord?

Him ye held less than the outer barbarian,
  Left him to die in his ignorant sin;
Have you no principles, humanitarian?
  Have you no precept—'Go gather them in?'

Knew he God's name? In his brutal profanity,
  That name was an oath—out of many but one.
What did he get from our famed Christianity?
  Where has his soul—if he had any—gone?

Fourteen years old, and what was he taught of it?
  What did he know of God's infinite Grace?
Draw the dark curtain of shame o'er the thought
    of it,
  Draw the shroud over the jockey-boy's face.

Bulletin, 26 February 1887

CONCERNING A STEEPLECHASE RIDER

Of all the ways in which men get a living there is none
so hard and so precarious as that of steeplechase-riding
in Australia. It is bad enough in England, where steeple-
chases only take place in winter, when the ground is
soft, where the horses are properly schooled before being
raced, and where most of the obstacles will yield a little
if struck and give the horse a chance to blunder over
safely.

In Australia the men have to go at racing-speed, on
very hard ground, over the most rigid and uncompromis-
ing obstacles—ironbark rails clamped into solid posts with
bands of iron. No wonder they are always coming to grief,
and are always in and out of hospital in splints and
bandages. Sometimes one reads that a horse has fallen
and the rider has 'escaped with a severe shaking'.

That 'shaking', gentle reader, would lay you or me up
for weeks, with a doctor to look after us and a crowd of
sympathetic friends calling to know how our poor back
was. But the steeplechase-rider has to be out and about
again, 'riding exercise' every morning, and 'schooling' all
sorts of cantankerous brutes over the fences. These men
take their lives in their hands and look at grim death
between their horses' ears every time they race or 'school'.

The death-record among Australian cross-country
jockeys and horses is very great; it is a curious instance
of how custom sanctifies all things that such horse-and-
man slaughter is accepted in such a callous way. If any
theatre gave a show at which men and horses were
habitually crippled or killed in full sight of the audience,
the manager would be put on his trial for manslaughter.

Our race-tracks use up their yearly average of horses
and men without attracting remark. One would sup-
pose that the risk being so great the profits were enor-
mous; but they are not. In 'the game' as played on our

racecourses there is just a bare living for a good capable horseman while he lasts, with the certainly of an ugly smash if he keeps at it long enough.

And they don't need to keep at it very long. After a few good 'shakings' they begin to take a nip or two to put heart into them before they go out, and after a while they have to increase the dose. At last they cannot ride at all without a regular cargo of alcohol on board, and are either 'half-muzzy' or shaky according as they have taken too much or too little.

Then the game becomes suicidal; it is an axiom that as soon as a man begins to funk he begins to fall. The reason is that a rider who has lost his nerve is afraid of his horse making a mistake, and takes a pull, or urges him onward, just at the crucial moment when the horse is rattling up to his fence and judging his distance. That little, nervous pull at his head or that little touch of the spur takes his attention from the fence, with the result that he makes his spring a foot too far off or a foot too close in, and— smash!

The loafers who hang about the big fences rush up to see if the jockey is killed or stunned; if he is, they dispose of any jewellery he may have about him; they have been known almost to tear a finger off in their endeavours to secure a ring. The ambulance clatters up at a canter, the poor rider is pushed in out of sight, and the ladies in the stand say how unlucky they are—that brute of a horse falling after they backed him. A wolfish-eyed man in the Leger-stand shouts to a wolfish-eyed pal, 'Bill, I believe that jock was killed when the chestnut fell,' and Bill replies, 'Yes, damn him, I had five bob on him.' And the rider, gasping like a crushed chicken, is carried into the casualty-room and laid on a little stretcher, while outside the window the bookmakers are roaring 'Four to one bar one,' and the racing is going on merrily as ever.

These remarks serve to introduce one of the fraternity

who may be considered as typical of all. He was a small, wiry, hard-featured fellow, the son of a stockman on a big cattle-station, and began life as a horse-breaker; he was naturally a horseman, able and willing to ride anything that could carry him. He left the station to go with cattle on the road, and, having picked up a horse that showed pace, amused himself by jumping over fences. Then he went to Wagga, entered the horse in a steeple-chase, rode him himself, won handsomely, sold the horse at a good price to a Sydney buyer, and went down to ride it in his Sydney races.

In Sydney he did very well; he got a name as a fearless and clever rider, and was offered several mounts on fine animals. So he pitched his camp in Sydney, and became a fully-enrolled member of the worst profession in the world. I had known him in the old days on the road, and when I met him on the course one day I enquired how he liked the new life.

'Well, it's a livin',' he said, 'but it's no great shakes. They don't give steeplechase-riders a chance in Sydney. There's very few faces, and the big sweepstakes keep horses out of the game.'

'Do you get a fair share of the riding?' I asked.

'Oh, yes; I get as much as anybody. But there's a lot of 'em got a notion I won't take hold of a horse when I'm told (i.e., pull him to prevent him winning). Some of these days I'll take hold of a horse when they don't expect it.'

I smiled as I thought there was probably a sorry day in store for some backer when the jockey 'took hold' unexpectedly.

'Do you have to pull horses, then, to get employment?'

'Oh, well, it's this way,' he said, rather apologetically, 'if an owner is badly treated by the handicapper, and is just giving his horse a run to get weight off, then it's right enough to catch hold a bit. But when a horse is favourite and the public are backing him it isn't right to take hold of him then. I would not do it.' This was his whole code of morals—not to pull a favourite; and he felt himself very superior to the scoundrel who would pull favourites or outsiders indiscriminately.

'What do you get for riding?' I asked him.

'Well,' he said, looking about uneasily, 'we're supposed to get a fiver for a losing mount and ten pounds if we win, but a lot of the steeplechase-owners are what I call "battlers"—men who have no money and get along by owing everybody. They promise us all sorts of money if we win, but they don't pay if we lose. I only got two pounds for that last steeplechase.'

'Two pounds!' I made a rapid calculation. He had ridden over eighteen fences for two pounds—had chanced his life eighteen times at less than half-a-crown a time.

'Good Heavens!' I said, 'that's a poor game. Wouldn't you be better back on the station?'

'Oh, I don't know—sometimes we get laid a bit to nothing, and do well out of a race. And then, you know, a steeplechase rider is somebody—not like an ordinary fellow that is just working.'

I realised that I was an 'ordinary fellow who was just working' and felt small accordingly.

'I'm just off to weigh now,' he said—'I'm riding Contractor, and he'll run well, but he always seems to fall at those logs. Still, I ought to have luck to-day. I met a hearse as I was coming out. I'll get him over the fences, somehow.'

'Do you think it lucky, then, to meet a hearse?'

'Oh, yes,' he said, 'if you *meet* it. You mustn't overtake it—that's unlucky. So is a cross-eyed man unlucky. Cross-eyed men ought to be kept off racecourses.'

He reappeared clad in his racing rig, and we set off to see the horse saddled. We found the owner in a great state of excitement. It seemed he had no money—absolutely none whatever—but had borrowed enough to pay the sweepstakes, and stood to make something if the horse won and lose nothing if he lost, as he had nothing to lose. My friend insisted on being paid two pounds before he would mount, and the owner nearly had a fit in his efforts to persuade him to ride on credit. At last a backer of the horse agreed to pay £2 10s., win or lose, and the rider was to get £25 out of the prize if he won. So up he got; and as he and the others walked the big muscular horses round the ring, nodding gaily to friends in the crowd, I thought of the gladiators going out to fight in the arena with the cry of 'Hail, Caesar, those about to die salute thee!'

The story of the race is soon told. My friend went to the front at the start and led nearly all the way, and 'Contractor!' was on everyone's lips as the big horse sailed along in front of his field. He came at the log-fence full of running, and it looked certain that he would get over. But at the last stride he seemed to falter, then plunged right into the fence, striking it with his chest, and, turning right over, landed on his unfortunate rider.

A crowd clustered round and hid horse and rider from view, and I ran down to the casualty-room to meet him when the ambulance came in. The limp form was carefully taken out and laid on a stretcher while a doctor examined the crushed ribs, the broken arm, and all the havoc that the horse's huge weight had wrought.

There was no hope from the first. My poor friend, who had so often faced death for two pounds, lay very still awhile. Then he began to talk, wandering in his mind. 'Where are the cattle?'—his mind evidently going back to the old days on the road. Then, quickly, 'Look out there—give me room!' and again 'Five-and-twenty pounds, Mary, and a sure thing if he don't fall at the logs.'

Mary was sobbing beside the bed, cursing the fence and the money that had brought him to grief. At last, in a tone of satisfaction, he said, quite clear and loud: 'I know how it was—there couldn't have been any dead man in that hearse!'

And so, having solved the mystery to his own satisfaction, he drifted away into unconsciousness—and woke somewhere on the other side of the big fence that we can neither see through nor over, but all have to face sooner or later.

> First published in the *Bulletin*,
> 12 December 1896. This version
> appeared in the collection titled
> *Three Elephant Power*, published
> in 1917.

TOMMY CORRIGAN

(Killed, Steeplechasing at Flemington.)

You talk of riders on the flat, of nerve and pluck
    and pace—
Not one in fifty has the nerve to ride a steeplechase.
It's right enough, while horses pull and take their
    fences strong,
To rush a flier to the front and bring the field along;
But what about the last half-mile, with horses blown
    and beat—
When every jump means all you know to keep him
    on his feet.

When any slip means sudden death—with wife and
    child to keep—
It needs some nerve to draw the whip and flog him
    at the leap—
But Corrigan would ride them out, by danger un-
    dismayed,
He never flinched at fence or wall, he never was
    afraid;

With easy seat and nerve of steel, light hand and
  smiling face,
He held the rushing horses back, and made the
  sluggards race.

He gave the shirkers extra heart, he steadied down
  the rash,
He rode great clumsy boring brutes, and chanced a
  fatal smash;
He got the rushing Wymlet home that never jumped
  at all—
But clambered over every fence and clouted every
  wall.
You should have heard the cheers, my boys, that
  shook the members' stand
Whenever Tommy Corrigan weighed out to ride
  Lone Hand.

They were, indeed, a glorious pair—the great up-
  standing horse,
The gamest jockey on his back that ever faced a
  course.
Though weight was big and pace was hot and
  fences stiff and tall,
'You follow Tommy Corrigan' was passed to one
  and all.
And every man on Ballarat raised all he could
  command
To put on Tommy Corrigan when riding old Lone
  Hand.

But now we'll keep his memory green while horse-
  men come and go;
We may not see his like again where silks and
  satins glow.

We'll drink to him in silence, boys—he's followed down
    the track
Where many a good man went before, but never one
    came back.
And, let us hope, in that far land where the shades of
    brave men reign,
The gallant Tommy Corrigan will ride Lone Hand
    again.

Bulletin, 18 August 1894

FATHER RILEY'S HORSE

'Twas the horse thief, Andy Regan, that was hunted
    like a dog
  By the troopers of the Upper Murray side;
They had searched in every gully, they had looked
    in every log,
  But never sight or track of him they spied,
Till the priest at Kiley's Crossing heard a knocking
    very late
  And a whisper 'Father Riley—come across!'
So his Reverence, in pyjamas, trotted softly to the
    gate
  And admitted Andy Regan—and a horse!

'Now, it's listen, Father Riley, to the words I've got
    to say,
  For it's close upon my death I am to-night.
With the troopers hard behind me I've been hiding
    all the day
  In the gullies keeping close and out of sight.
But they're watching all the ranges till there's not
    a bird could fly,
  And I'm fairly worn to pieces with the strife,

So I'm taking no more trouble, but I'm going home
to die,
   'Tis the only way I see to save my life.

'Yes, I'm making home to mother's, and I'll die on
Tuesday next
   An' be buried on the Thursday—and, of course,
I'm prepared to do my penance; but with one thing
I'm perplexed
   And it's—Father, it's this jewel of a horse!
He was never bought nor paid for, and there's not a
man can swear
   To his owner or his breeder, but I know
That his sire was by Pedantic from the Old Pre-
tender mare,
   And his dam was close related to The Roe.

'And there's nothing in the district that can race
him for a step—
   He could canter while they're going at their top:
He's the king of all the leppers that was ever seen
to lep;
   A five-foot fence—he'd clear it in a hop!
So I'll leave him with you, Father, till the dead
shall rise again,
   'Tis yourself that knows a good un; and, of
course,
You can say he's got by Moonlight out of Paddy
Murphy's plain
   If you're ever asked the breeding of the horse!

'But it's getting on to daylight, and it's time to say
good-bye.
   For the stars above the East are growing pale.
And I'm making home to mother—and it's hard for
me to die!
   But it's harder still, is keeping out of gaol!

You can ride the old horse over to my grave across
    the dip,
  Where the wattle-bloom is waving overhead.
Sure he'll jump them fences easy—you must never
    raise the whip
  Or he'll rush 'em!—now, good-bye!' and he had
    fled!

So they buried Andy Regan, and they buried him to
    rights,
  In the graveyard at the back of Kiley's Hill;
There were five-and-twenty mourners who had five-
    and-twenty fights
  Till the very boldest fighters had their fill.
There were fifty horses racing from the graveyard
    to the pub,
  And the riders flogged each other all the while—
And the lashins of the liquor! And the lavins of
    the grub!
  Oh, poor Andy went to rest in proper style.

Then the races came to Kiley's—with a steeplechase
    and all,
  For the folk were mostly Irish round about,
And it takes an Irish rider to be fearless of a fall;
  They were training morning in and morning out.
But they never started training till the sun was on
    the course.
  For a superstitious story kept 'em back.
That the ghost of Andy Regan on a slashing chest-
    nut horse
  Had been training by the starlight on the track.

And they read the nominations for the races with
    surprise
  And amusement at the Father's little joke,

For a novice had been entered for the steeplechasing
    prize,
  And they found that it was Father Riley's moke!
He was neat enough to gallop, he was strong enough
    to stay!
  But his owner's views of training were immense,
For the Reverend Father Riley used to ride him
    every day,
  And he never saw a hurdle nor a fence.

And the priest would join the laughter; 'Oh,' said
    he, 'I put him in,
  For there's five-and-twenty sovereigns to be won;
And the poor would find it useful if the chestnut
    chanced to win,
  As he'll maybe do when all is said and done!'
He had called him Faugh-a-ballagh (which is French
    for 'Clear the course'),
  And his colours were a vivid shade of green:
All the Dooleys and O'Donnells were on Father
    Riley's horse,
  While the Orangemen were backing Mandarin!

It was Hogan, the dog-poisoner—aged man and very
    wise,
  Who was camping in the racecourse with his swag,
And who ventured the opinion, to the township's
    great surprise,
  That the race would go to Father Riley's nag.
'You can talk about your riders—and the horse has
    not been schooled,
  And the fences is terrific, and the rest!
When the field is fairly going, then ye'll see ye've all
    been fooled.
  And the chestnut horse will battle with the best.

'For there's some has got condition, and they think
    the race is sure,
  And the chestnut horse will fall beneath the
    weight;
But the hopes of all the helpless, and the prayers of
    all the poor,
  Will be running by his side to keep him straight.
And it's what's the need of schoolin' or of workin'
    on the track,
  Whin the Saints are there to guide him round the
    course!
I've prayed him over every fence—I've prayed him
    out and back!
  And I'll bet my cash on Father Riley's horse!'

      •   •   •

Oh, the steeple was a caution! They went tearin'
    round and round,
  And the fences rang and rattled where they struck.
There was some that cleared the water—there was
    more fell in and drowned—
Some blamed the men and others blamed the luck!
But the whips were flying freely when the field
    came into view
  For the finish down the long green stretch of
    course,
And in front of all the flyers, jumpin' like a
    kangaroo,
  Came the rank outsider—Father Riley's horse!

Oh, the shouting and the cheering as he rattled past
    the post!
  For he left the others standing, in the straight;
And the rider—well, they reckoned it was Andy
    Regan's ghost,
  And it beat 'em how a ghost would draw the
    weight!

But he weighed it, nine stone seven; then he laughed
    and disappeared,
  Like a Banshee (which is Spanish for an elf),
And old Hogan muttered sagely, 'If it wasn't for
    the beard
  They'd be thinking it was Andy Regan's self!'

And the poor of Kiley's Crossing drank the health
    at Christmastide
  Of the chestnut and his rider dressed in green.
There was never such a rider, not since Andy Regan
    died,
  And they wondered who on earth he could have
    been.
But they settled it among 'em, for the story got
    about,
  'Mongst the bushmen and the people on the
    course,
That the Devil had been ordered to let Andy Regan
    out
  For the steeplechase on Father Riley's horse!

Bulletin, 9 December 1899

THE ORACLE AT THE RACES

No tram ever goes to Randwick races without him; he is
always fat, hairy, and assertive; he is generally one of a
party, and he takes the centre of the stage all the time—
collects and hands over the fares, adjusts the change,
chaffs the conductor, crushes the thin, apologetic stranger
next to him into a pulp, and talks to the whole compart-
ment as if they had asked for his opinion.

He knows all the trainers and owners, or takes care to
give the impression that he does. He slowly and pomp-
ously hauls out his race book, and one of his satellites
opens the ball by saying, in a deferential way:

'What do you like for the 'urdles, Charley?'

The Oracle looks at the book, and breathes heavily; no one else ventures to speak.

'Well,' he says, at last, 'of course there's only one in it—if he's wanted. But that's it—will they spin him? I don't think they will. They's only a lot o' cuddies, any'ow.'

No one likes to expose his own ignorance by asking which horse he refers to as the 'only one in it'; and the Oracle goes on to deal out some more wisdom in a loud voice.

'Billy K—— told me' (he probably hardly knows Billy K—— by sight) 'Billy K—— told me that bay 'orse ran the best mile-an-'a-half ever done on Randwick yesterday; but I don't give him a chance, for all that; that's the worst of these trainers. They don't know when their horses are well—half of 'em.'

Then a voice comes from behind him. It is that of the thin man, who is crushed out of sight by the bulk of the Oracle.

'I think,' says the thin man, 'that that horse of Flannery's ought to run well in the Handicap.'

The Oracle can't stand this sort of thing at all. He gives a snort, wheels half-round and looks at the speaker. Then he turns back to the compartment full of people, and says: 'No 'ope.'

The thin man makes a last effort. 'Well, they backed him last night, anyhow.'

'Who backed 'im?' says the Oracle.

'In Tattersall's,' says the thin man.

'I'm sure,' says the Oracle; and the thin man collapses.

On arrival at the course, the Oracle is in great form. Attended by his string of satellites, he plods from stall to stall staring at the horses. Their names are printed in big letters on the stalls, but the Oracle doesn't let that stop his display of knowledge.

"Ere's Blue Fire,' he says, stopping at that animal's stall, and swinging his race book. 'Good old Blue Fire!' he

goes on loudly, as a little court collects. 'Jimmy B——'
(mentioning a popular jockey) 'told me he couldn't have
lost on Saturday week if he had only been ridden differ-
ent. I had a good stake on him, too, that day. Lor', the
races that has been chucked away on this horse. They
will not ride him right.'

A trainer who is standing by, civilly interposes. 'This
isn't Blue Fire,' he says. 'Blue Fire's out walking about.
This is a two-year-old filly that's in the stall—'

'Well, I can see that, can't I?' says the Oracle, crush-
ingly. 'You don't suppose I thought Blue Fire was a mare,
did you?' and he moves off hurriedly.

'Now, look here, you chaps,' he says to his followers at
last. 'You wait here. I want to go and see a few of the
talent, and it don't do to have a crowd with you. There's
Jimmy M—— over there now' (pointing to a leading
trainer). 'I'll get hold of him in a minute. He couldn't tell
me anything with so many about. Just you wait here.'

He crushes into a crowd that has gathered round the
favourite's stall, and overhears one hard-faced racing man
say to another, 'What do you like?' to which the other
answers, 'Well, either this or Royal Scot. I think I'll put
a bit on Royal Scot.' This is enough for the Oracle. He
doesn't know either of the men from Adam, or either of
the horses from the great original pachyderm, but the
information will do to go on with. He rejoins his followers,
and looks very mysterious.

'Well, did you hear anything?' they say.

The Oracle talks low and confidentially.

'The crowd that have got the favourite tell me they're
not afraid of anything but Royal Scot,' he says. 'I think
we'd better put a bit on both.'

'What did the Royal Scot crowd say?' asks an admirer
deferentially.

'Oh, they're going to try and win. I saw the stable
commissioner, and he told me they were going to put a
hundred on him. Of course, you needn't say I told you,

'cause I promised him I wouldn't tell.' And the satellites beam with admiration of the Oracle, and think what a privilege it is to go to the races with such a knowing man.

They contribute their mites to the general fund, some putting in a pound, others half a sovereign, and the Oracle takes it into the ring to invest, half on the favourite and half on Royal Scot. He finds that the favourite is at two to one, and Royal Scot at threes, eight to one being offered against anything else. As he ploughs through the ring, a Whisperer (one of those broken-down followers of the turf who get their living in various mysterious ways, but partly by giving 'tips' to backers) pulls his sleeve.

'What are you backing?' he says.

'Favourite and Royal Scot,' says the Oracle.

'Put a pound on Bendemeer,' says the tipster. 'It's a certainty. Meet me here if it comes off, and I'll tell you something for the next race. Don't miss it now. Get on quick!'

The Oracle is humble enough before the hanger-on of the turf. A bookmaker roars '10 to 1 Bendemeer'; he suddenly fishes out a sovereign of his own—and he hasn't money to spare, for all his knowingness—and puts it on Bendemeer. His friends' money he puts on the favourite and Royal Scot as arranged. Then they all go round to watch the race.

The horses are at the post; a distant cluster of crowded animals with little dots of colour on their backs. Green, blue, yellow, purple, French grey, and old gold, they change about in a bewildering manner, and though the Oracle has a cheap pair of glasses, he can't make out where Bendemeer has got to. Royal Scot and the favourite he has lost interest in, and secretly hopes that they will be left at the post or break their necks; but he does not confide his sentiment to his companions.

They're off! The long line of colours across the track becomes a shapeless clump and then draws out into a long string. 'What's that in front?' yells someone at the rails. 'Oh, that thing of Hart's,' says someone else. But the Oracle hears them not; he is looking in the mass of colour for a purple cap and grey jacket, with black arm bands. He cannot see it anywhere, and the confused and confusing mass swings round the turn into the straight.

Then there is a babel of voices, and suddenly a shout of 'Bendemeer! Bendemeer!' and the Oracle, without knowing which is Bendemeer, takes up the cry feverishly. 'Bendemeer! Bendemeer!' he yells, waggling his glasses about, trying to see where the animal is.

'Where's Royal Scot, Charley? Where's Royal Scot?' screams one of his friends, in agony. "Ow's he doin'?"

'No 'ope!' says the Oracle, with fiendish glee. 'Bendemeer! Bendemeer!'

The horses are at the Leger stand now, whips are out, and three horses seem to be nearly abreast; in fact, to the Oracle there seem to be a dozen nearly abreast. Then a big chestnut sticks his head in front of the others, and a small man at the Oracle's side emits a deafening series of yells right by the Oracle's ear:

'Go on, Jimmy! Rub it into him! Belt him! It's a cake-walk! A cake-walk!' The big chestnut, in a dogged sort of way, seems to stick his body clear of his opponents, and passes the post a winner by a length. The Oracle doesn't know what has won, but fumbles with his book. The number on the saddle-cloth catches his eye—No. 7; he looks hurriedly down the page. No. 7—Royal Scot. Second is No. 24—Bendemeer. Favourite nowhere.

Hardly has he realised it, before his friends are cheering and clapping him on the back. 'By George, Charley, it takes you to pick 'em.' 'Come and 'ave a wet!' 'You 'ad a quid in, didn't you, Charley?' The Oracle feels very sick at having missed the winner, but he dies game. 'Yes, rather; I had a quid on,' he says. 'And' (here he nerves himself to smile) 'I had a saver on the second, too.'

His comrades gasp with astonishment. 'D'you hear that, eh? Charley backed first and second. That's pickin' 'em if you like.' They have a wet, and pour fulsome adulation on the Oracle when he collects their money.

After the Oracle has collected the winnings for his friends he meets the Whisperer again.

'It didn't win?' he says to the Whisperer in inquiring tones.

'Didn't win,' says the Whisperer, who has determined to brazen the matter out. 'How could he win? Did you see the way he was ridden? That horse was stiffened just after I seen you, and he never tried a yard. Did you see the way he was pulled and hauled about at the turn? It'd make a man sick. What was the stipendiary stewards doing, I wonder?'

This fills the Oracle with a new idea. All that he remembers of the race at the turn was a jumble of colours, a kaleidoscope of horses and of riders hanging on to the horses' necks. But it wouldn't do to admit that he didn't see everything, and didn't know everything; so he plunges in boldly.

'O' course I saw it,' he says. 'And a blind man could see it. They ought to rub him out.'

'Course they ought,' says the Whisperer. 'But, look here, put two quid on Tell-tale; you'll get it all back!'

The Oracle does put on 'two quid', and doesn't get it all back. Neither does he see any more of this race than he did of the last one—in fact, he cheers wildly when the wrong horse is coming in. But when the public begin to hoot he hoots as loudly as anybody—louder if anything; and all the way home in the tram he lays down the law about stiff running, and wants to know what the stipendiaries are doing.

If you go into any barber's shop, you can hear him at it, and he flourishes in suburban railway carriages; but he has a tremendous local reputation, having picked first and second in the handicap, and it would be a bold man who would venture to question the Oracle's knowledge of racing and of all matters relating to it.

> First published in the *Evening News*,
> 30 January 1904. This version
> appeared in *Three Elephant Power*,
> 1917.

HINTS TO URGERS—HOW TO TELL THE TALE

The Methods of Napoleon

In the present dearth of employment the trade or profession of Urger offers an avenue of lucrative work to men with the necessary gifts.

Inquiry at the Mitchell Library has failed to discover any standard publication dealing with the profession of Urger, and there is no doubt that a reliable 'Urger's Guide' would meet with a successful sale.

Failing any publication of the sort, the following hints, compiled by a leading practitioner, may be found useful to those who follow this interesting and lucrative business.

1. Always be well dressed. Have everything on your back, even if you have nothing in your stomach.

2. Never allow your patients to have any opinion of their own. The Urger who argues with his patients is lost. He is in the same trouble as a Police Court attorney who allows his client to suggest the questions, or a doctor who allows the patient's mother-in-law to butt in.

3. Never give any reasons for your advice. If you tell a man to back a horse, tell him that it is unbeatable. No half measures are of any use.

4.   If the patient suggests that the horse ran badly last time, do not argue with him. Say 'He's home and dried.' If he persists in his argument, say 'He'll lob in.' Once you admit any doubt in your own mind the patient will lose confidence in you.

5.   If your tip is beaten and you have to 'tell the tale' after the race, never say that the horse was stiff. The patient will lose faith in you for putting him to a stiff 'un. Say, 'Of course, you saw what happened to him at the back!' It is a thousand to one that he did not see anything but he would sooner die than admit it.

6.   If the horse you have tipped starts to drift in the market, your patient will require building up a bit. Tell him that the big punters are in on your tip long ago, and that the fool public are now backing the other horses, causing yours to lengthen in price.

7.   Never appear too anxious to get a patient in on a horse. Tell him that the right people are going to back a stone certainty, and that as a favour you can let him have a little in with them, but not too much or he will spoil the market. Make a favour of it.

8.   Don't make yourself too cheap. Your methods should always be Napoleonic. If the patient is inclined to hesitate, tell him to stop where he is and not to move a yard or speak to anybody till you go and see the jockey's brother. Then you can go and have a pie and a cup of tea and when you come back you will find the patient rooted to the spot where you left him. Tell him it is unbeatable and the rest is easy.

By attention to these details and the cultivation of a good bedside manner, you should be able to build up a large and lucrative practice.

Sydney Sportsman, 19 September 1922

SHAKESPEARE ON THE TURF
AN UNPUBLISHED DRAMA
A WINTER'S TURF TALE

*[As the public have 'stood' uncomplainingly the publication
of a portrait of the Supreme Being, they may accept the follow-
ing drama as the work of William Shakespeare.]*

ACT I

Scene I

The saddling paddock at a racecourse.

*Citizens, Battlers, Toffs, Trainers, Flappers, Satyrs,
Bookmakers and Turf Experts.*

Enter Shortinbras, a Trainer, and two Punters.

FIRST PUNTER: Good Shortinbras, what thinkest thou
of the Fav'rite!

SHORTINBRAS (*aside*): This poltroon would not venture
a ducat on David to beat a dead donkey; a dull and
muddy-mettled rascal.

(*To Punter*): Aye marry Sir, I think well of the Favourite.

PUNTER:

And yet I have a billiard marker's word

That in this race to-day they back Golumpus.

And when they bet, they tell me, they will knock

The favourite for a string of German Sausage.

SHORTINBRAS:

Aye, marry, they would tell thee, I've no doubt,

It is the way of owners that they tell

To billiard markers and the men on trams

Just when they mean to bet. Go back it, back it!

(*Tries to shuffle off, but Punter detains him.*)

PUNTER: Nay, good Shortinbras, what thinkest thou of
Golumpus? Was it not dead last week?

SHORTINBRAS: Marry, Sir, I think well of Golumpus.
'Tis safer to speak well of the dead: betimes they rise
again.

(*Sings*)

They pulled him barefaced in the mile,

Hey, Nonny, Nonny.

The Stipes were watching them all the while;
And the losers swear, but the winners smile,
  Hey, Nonny, Nonny.
                    Exit Shortinbras.

SECOND PUNTER:

A scurvy Knave! What meant he by his prate
Of Fav'rite and outsider and the like?
Forsooth he told us nothing. Follow him close.
Give him good watch, I pray you, till we see
Just what he does his dough on. Follow fast.
                    Exeunt Punters.

Scene II

The same. Bookmakers call: 'Seven to Four on the Field!'
'Three to One, Bar One! Ten to One, Golumpus.'
  Enter Two Heads.

FIRST HEAD:

How goes the Battle? Didst thou catch the last?

SECOND HEAD:

Aye, marry did I, and the one before;
But this has got me beat. The favourite drifts,
And not a single wager has been laid
About Golumpus. Thinkest thou that both are dead?
  Re-enter Punters.

PUNTER:

Good morrow, Gentlemen. I have it cold
Straight from the owner, that Golumpus goes
Eyes out to win to-day.

FIRST HEAD:

Prate not to me of owners. Hast thou seen
The good red gold go in. The Jockey's Punter
Has he put up the stuff, or does he wait
To get a better price. Owner, say'st thou?
The owner does the paying, and the talk;
Hears the tale afterwards when it gets beat
And sucks it in as hungry babes suck milk.
Look you how ride the books in motor cars

While owners go on foot, or ride in trams,
Crushed with the vulgar herd and doomed to hear
From mouths of striplings that their horse was stiff.
When they themselves are broke with backing it.

Scene III

Enter an Owner and a Jockey.

OWNER: 'Tis a good horse. A passing good horse
JOCKEY:

I rode him yesternoon: it seemed to me
That in good truth a fairly speedy cow
Might well out-run him.

OWNER:

Thou froward varlet; Must I say again
That on the Woop Woop course he ran a mile
In less than forty with his irons on!

JOCKEY: Then thou should'st bring the Woop Woop course down here.

OWNER: Thou pestilential scurvy Knave. Go to!
Strikes him.

Alarms and excursions. The race is run and Shortinbras enters, leading in the winner.

FIRST PUNTER:

And thou hast trained the winner, thou thyself,
Thou complicated liar. Did'st not say
To back Golumpus or the Favourite!

SHORTINBRAS:

Get work! For all I ever had of thee.
My children were unfed, my wife unclothed,
And I myself condemned to menial toil.

PUNTER:

The man who keeps a winner to himself
Deserves but death. (Kills him).

Enter defeated Owner and Jockey.

OWNER:

Thou whoreson Knave: thou went into a trance
Soon as the barrier lifted and knew nought

Of what occurred until they neared the post.
(Kills him).
Curtain falls on ensemble of punters, bookmakers, heads
and surviving jockeys and trainers.
CURTAIN.

Sydney Sportsman, 6 May 1923

The Reporter's Eye

*... the sufferer's face grows an ashen grey. The doctor
hurries off, and you are left along with the dying man ...
(A Day Under Fire)*

It's hard to fit Paterson's first effort, 'El Mahdi to the Australian Troops', into any category, so somewhat arbitrarily I've put it with the South African pieces. Likewise the venture into South American political commentary, *The Boss of the* Admiral Lynch, is placed here.

The last piece on the dog-poisoner was published in the *Sydney Sportsman* in 1922. It is sad that in the remaining years no publisher or editor got Paterson to write more prose on outback people and types in place of dull pieces on irrigation and so on.

EL MAHDI TO THE AUSTRALIAN TROOPS

And wherefore have they come, this war-like band,
That o'er the ocean many a weary day
Have tossed; and now beside Suakim's Bay,
  With faces stern and resolute, do stand,
Waking the desert's echoes with the drum—
Men of Australia, wherefore have ye come?

To keep the Puppet Khedive on his throne,
To strike a blow for tyranny and wrong,
To crush the weak and aid the oppressing strong!
  Regardless of the hapless Fellah's moan,
To force the payment of the Hebrew loan,
Squeezing the tax like blood from out the stone?

And fair Australia, freest of the free,
is up in arms against the freeman's fight;
And with her mother joined to crush the right—
  Has left her threatened treasures o'er the sea,
Has left her land of liberty and law
To flesh her maiden sword in this unholy war.

Enough! God never blessed such enterprise—
England's degenerate Generals yet shall rue
Brave Gordon sacrificed, when soon they view
  The children of a thousand deserts rise
To drive them forth like sand before the gale—
God and the Prophet! Freedom will prevail.

                                        El Mahdi

                    Bulletin, 28 February 1885

THE BOSS OF THE *ADMIRAL LYNCH*

Did you ever hear tell of Chili? I was readin' the
    other day
Of President Balmaceda and of how he was sent
    away.
It seems that he didn't suit 'em—they thought that
    they'd like a change,
So they started an insurrection and chased him
    across the range.
They seem to be restless people—and, judging
    by what you hear,
They raise up these revolutions 'bout two or three
    times a year;
And the man that goes out of office, he goes
    for the boundary quick,
For there isn't no vote by ballot—it's bullets that
    does the trick.
And it ain't like a real battle, where the prisoners'
    lives are spared,
And they fight till there's one side beaten and then
    there's truce declared,
And the man that has got the licking goes down
    like a blooming lord
To hand in his resignation and give up his bloom-
    ing sword,
And the other man bows and takes it, and every-
    thing's all polite—
This wasn't that sort of a picnic, this wasn't that
    sort of a fight.
For the pris'ners they took—they shot 'em, no odds
    were they small or great;
If they'd collared old Balmaceda, they reckoned to
    shoot him straight.
A lot of bloodthirsty devils they were—but there
    ain't a doubt

They must have been real plucked uns, the way
    that they fought it out,
And the king of 'em all, I reckon, the man that
    could stand a pinch,
Was the boss of a one-horse gunboat. They called
    her the *Admiral Lynch*.
Well, he was for Balmaceda, and after the war was
    done,
And Balmaceda was beaten and his troops had been
    forced to run,
The other man fetched his army and proceeded to do
    things brown.
He marched 'em into the fortress and took command
    of the town,
Cannon and guns and horses troopin' along the road,
Rumblin' over the bridges; and never a foeman showed
Till they came in sight of the harbour—and the
    very first thing they see
Was this mite of a one-horse gunboat a-lying against
    the quay;
And there as they watched they noticed a flutter of
    crimson rag,
And under their eyes he hoisted old Balmaceda's flag.
Well, I tell you it fairly knocked 'em—it just took
    away their breath,
For he must ha' known if they caught him, 'twas
    nothin' but sudden death.
An' he'd got no fire in his furnace, no chance to
    put out to sea,
So he stood by his gun and waited with his vessel
    against the quay.
Well, they sent him a civil message to say that the
    war was done,
And most of his side were corpses, and all that were
    left had run,

And blood had been spilt sufficient; so they gave
    him a chance to decide
If he'd haul down his bit of bunting and come on
    the winning side.
He listened and heard their message, and answered
    them all polite
That he was a Spanish hidalgo, and the men of his
    race *must* fight!
A gunboat against an army, and with never a chance
    to run,
And them with their hundred cannon and him with
    a single gun:
The odds were a trifle heavy—but he wasn't the sort
    to flinch,
So he opened fire on the army, did the boss of the
    Admiral Lynch.
They pounded his boat to pieces, they silenced his
    single gun,
And captured the whole consignment, for none of
    'em cared to run;
And it don't say whether they shot him—it don't
    even give his name—
But whatever they did I'll wager that he went to
    his graveyard game.
I tell you those old hidalgos so stately and so polite,
They turn out the real Maginnis when it comes to
    an uphill fight.
There was General Alcantara, who died in the
    heaviest brunt,
And General Alzereca was killed in the battle's front;
But the king of 'em all, I reckon—the man that
    could stand a pinch—
Was the man who attacked the army with the gun-
    boat *Admiral Lynch*.

Bulletin, 10 December 1892

THE PEARL DIVER

Kanzo Makame, the diver, sturdy and small Japanee,
Seeker of pearls and of pearl-shell down in the depths
of the sea,
Trudged o'er the bed of the ocean, searching
industriously.

Over the pearl-grounds the lugger drifted—a little
white speck:
Joe Nagasaki, the 'tender', holding the life-line on
deck,
Talked through the rope to the diver, knew when to
drift or to check.

Kanzo was king of his lugger, master and diver in
one,
Diving wherever it pleased him, taking instructions
from none;
Hither and thither he wandered, steering by stars
and by sun.

Fearless he was beyond credence, looking at death
eye to eye:
This was his formula always, 'All man go dead by
and by—
S'posing time come no can help it—s'pose time no
come, then no die.'

Dived in the depths of the Darnleys, down twenty
fathom and five;
Down where by law, and by reason, men are for-
bidden to dive;
Down in a pressure so awful that only the strongest
survive:

Sweated four men at the air pumps, fast as the
    handles could go,
Forcing the air down that reached him heated and
    tainted, and slow—
Kanzo Makame the diver stayed seven minutes below;

Came up on deck like a dead man, paralysed body
    and brain;
Suffered, while blood was returning, infinite tortures
    of pain:
Sailed once again to the Darnleys—laughed and
    descended again!

      •   •   •

Scarce grew the shell in the shallows, rarely a patch
    could they touch;
Always the take was so little, always the labour so
    much;
Always they thought of the Islands held by the
    lumbering Dutch—

Islands where shell was in plenty lying in passage
    and bay,
Islands where divers could gather hundreds of shell
    in a day:
But the lumbering Dutch in their gunboats they
    hunted the divers away.

Joe Nagasaki, the 'tender', finding the profits grow
    small,
Said, 'Let us go to the Islands, try for a number
    one haul!
If we get caught, go to prison—let them take lugger
    and all!'

Kanzo Makame, the diver—knowing full well what
    it meant—
Fatalist, gambler, and stoic, smiled a broad smile of
    content,

Flattened in mainsail and foresail, and off to the
    Islands they went.

Close to the headlands they drifted, picking up shell
    by the ton,
Piled up on deck were the oysters, opening wide in
    the sun,
When, from the lee of the headland, boomed the
    report of a gun.

Then if the diver was sighted, pearl-shell and lugger
    must go—
Joe Nagasaki decided (quick was the word and the
    blow),
Cut both the pipe and the life-line, leaving the diver
    below!

Kanzo Makame, the diver, failing to quite understand,
Pulled the 'haul up' on the life-line, found it was
    slack in his hand;
Then, like a little brown stoic, lay down and died on
    the sand.

Joe Nagasaki, the 'tender', smiling a sanctified smile,
Headed her straight for the gunboat—throwing out
    shells all the while—
Then went aboard and reported, 'No makee dive in
    three mile!'

'Dress no have got and no helmet—diver go shore
    on the spree;
Plenty wind come and break rudder—lugger get blown
    out to sea:
Take me to Japanee Consul, he help a poor
    Japanee!'

•   •   •

So the Dutch let him go; but they watched him, as
  off from the Islands he ran,
Doubting him much—but what would you? You have
  to be sure of your man
Ere you wake up that nest-full of hornets—the little
  brown men of Japan.

Down in the ooze and the coral, down where earth's
  wonders are spread,
Helmeted, ghastly, and swollen, Kanzo Makame lies
  dead.
Joe Nagasaki, his 'tender', is owner and diver instead.

Wearer of pearls in your necklace, comfort yourself
  if you can.
These are the risks of the pearling—these are the
  ways of Japan;
'Plenty more Japanee diver, plenty more little brown
  man!'

Rio Grande's Last Race, 1902

A Trip with the Pearlers

Arrived at Thursday Island on a vessel from London.
Spent the evening ashore; an inferno of drink and sweat.
One of the ship's stewards (an Englishman) went ashore
to enjoy himself on the tips collected during the voyage;
he tried to go the pace of Thursday Island and was car-
ried aboard in a fit alcoholic in about two hours.

We went to a Cingalese opera in which the hero, a
coloured sportsman, in what looked like a Dutch uniform
but with knee breeches and very very thin legs, sang in
monotonous cadence to another man dressed as a woman.
The origin of the play was apparently Dutch, as the book
of the words said that the hero and heroine escaped to
Holland and lived happily ever after. The audience was

various in colour and nationality, and when we asked if there were any room in the front seats we were told that there was not much room as four gentlemen had gone in already.

Having 'done' the opera we went round the town and found plenty of incident. All the pearling luggers were in for refitting and the crews were spending their money. One Malay had a row with an acquaintance and promptly swiped a knife into him, and there was much yelling and shouting till he was captured and locked up. The two police, by the way, claim to hold the Australian record, having arrested 18 drunks in 7 minutes.

A Manila man whose attentions had been scorned by a barmaid pulled a revolver on a successful rival and put one bullet into the leg of a Japanese bystander and another into a decanter of gin. Then he fled but the two local 'Johns' surrounded him and arrested him in the most matter of fact way, and put him in with the inebriates.

These coloured people fight among themselves, but are very much in awe of the police; which is just as well, for they are free with the knife and indiscriminate with the revolver.

The town was full of life and movement, gambling going on everywhere. A merry-go-round and a swinging-boat outfit were doing a roaring business, and at the Japanese end of the town was the tinkle of the little Japanese fiddler, and the songs of the Jap women who sat out on the verandahs and charmed passersby as the sirens charmed Ulysses.

Out on a Schooner

After seeing all the sights of Thursday Island the next thing was to get away on a pearling lugger and in this land of unlimited hospitality that was soon fixed up. A schooner was going out to the fleet and we could go in her. Followed a hurried packing of necessaries, and we went down to the jetty and found a beautiful little schooner of 40 tons built by the Langfords in Sydney, with white decks and white sails. This, it turned out, was a 'tender' to the supply schooner which accompanies each pearling fleet. The supply schooner carries supplies of all sorts, spare diving gear, food and clothing, etc., etc. The tender is a smaller schooner that sails out to the fleet and back with shell.

Once on board the lugger—or rather the tender—sails were hoisted and we were off. The ship's company consisted of two white men, both Queenslanders, both fine men physically. The captain had been a sailor and a shipwright, and had then taken up diving. His mate was a Hercules in build, and right through Northern Queensland you will find as fine men physically as anywhere in Australia. In other tropical countries one finds weeds, yellow-faced unhealthy men, but these Queenslanders are as fine a race of men as can be found anywhere. Probably the weaklings die off or get full of it and make for civilisation.

The crew were three Malays and an Australian coast-black from Murray Island, a very big powerful binghi with a good deal of Papuan or Malayan blood in him. The crew had just had their leave ashore and had gambled away every red cent they had in the world. They gamble at poker, of all games in the world!

We sailed in a light wind and made poor progress—sailing three miles in one direction and drifting five miles in another, till at last we caught a favourable tide rip, and after a day of lazy sailing we came to the fleet at anchor.

Supply Schooner and Tender

A pearling fleet consists of a supply schooner and a dozen or so of luggers. The particular supply schooner that we boarded was a big roomy vessel of 180 tons, 99 feet long by 23 feet beam, and her ship's company were as mixed a crowd as one could find anywhere in the world. A white man was of course in charge and he had a white mate, but the crew were of all nationalities. The pearling luggers were anchored around the schooner like chickens around a hen and their crews were all on board the schooner gossipping and gambling. There were Manila men, American niggers, Australian coast-blacks, ditto mainlanders, Japanese, New Guinea men and South Sea Islanders, Javanese, Malays, which means Singapore and Archipelago men, as distinguished from Manila men, and a few half breeds. There was even one Portugoose—all through the east anything black and doubtful of origin is a Portugoose.

They could not any of them talk another nation's language, so they conversed in Pidgin English: 'Me you go walkabout', 'Where that fellow bucket sit down?' etc., etc. These lugger crews do the actual diving, and the diver, whether Malay, Japanese or Manila man, is always the navigator. They have no master certificates, no knowledge of navigation, no idea of using the compass. They simply go by some unerring instinct and go quite straight. If a man were to say to his diver, 'Take the lugger to New Guinea,' you would see him set her nose straight forward, and they get there all right. Always in the lugger there are men who have been there before— they have been everywhere for that matter. The insurance companies will insure the luggers, though they are not navigated by ticketed men, though some of the Japs are navigators, and can use the sextant.

A Captain's Troubles

The Captain of the supply schooner made us welcome and told us he was making ready for another cruise after shell. 'Here's this cook,' he said, pointing to a yellow-faced shock haired nondescript. 'He signed on for two years and got ten pounds advance to buy his outfit. He

goes off to T.I. (Thursday Island) and comes back as
naked as a b—— y robin. The first thing he bought for
his outfit was two bottles of champagne and that's all he
remembers!' The lugger hands kept coming up for sup-
plies: 'Altogether boy want pineapple', 'Altogether boy
want bissikit'. The New Guinea boys were not allowed to
draw any slop chest luxuries, as their money had to be
accounted for and paid over in New Guinea, but by an
unwritten law they got tinned pineapple, ginger beer and
biscuits once a week.

While the fleet was at anchor we got a lugger and crew
and sailed off in search of adventure. We sailed past a
beach of white sand, and saw the track where a turtle
had gone ashore to lay her eggs, and one of the coast-
blacks, after prodding the sand with a sharp pointed
stick, dug up the eggs, which they regard as great luxur-
ies. Then we sailed on and landed at Jardine Station on
the peninsular and a turkey hunt was next in order.
Why is it that misfortune always dogs the steps of ama-
teur sportsmen? A black fellow was told off to go and get
the turkey dog and he never said that the turkey dog
was away with the gins. No, he just set off quite gaily
and walked seven miles or so after the gins, and when he
got to them the turkey dog would not follow him, so the
turkey shoot was a fiasco. We tramped and tramped and
tramped through the jungle, and the lawyer vines cut
us and the green ants fell from the boughs and bit us,
and we only saw one turkey and he was flying like an
aeroplane through the trees. But these disappointments
are all in the day's work.

Beating back to the schooner one of the men, an old
island native, rather surprised us by bursting out crying.
'What for you cry?' said the Captain. 'I feel no good.'
'What for you feel no good?' 'I see plenty island, plenty
place a long time ago, all my people—plenty people. Now
where all gone? All gone dead. Melly (very) few people
now.'

It made us all feel 'no good' too.

Legislation has cut out a lot of the coloured labour, but the pearling fleet still work and any man wanting a holiday can get sport and a little excitement by taking on a holiday trip in a lugger. One interstate sea captain put in his holiday this way and got a £900 pearl. While he was showing it to an acquaintance on board the lugger in Darwin Harbour the pearl slipped from his fingers and bounced overboard. A diver was sent down and recovered the pearl from the bottom and the captain never let it on deck again till he disposed of it to a local dealer. Any party of sportsmen who had a couple of months holiday could make a fairly inexpensive and very interesting trip in a lugger in northern waters. The diving itself is an experience well worth going through, and there is always the chance of finding a good pearl. If this pearling business were run in American waters it would attract tourists in hundreds, and there are plenty of people in Australia who have the necessary money to take what is after all not a very long or very expensive trip.

The *Sydney Sportsman*, 15 May 1923

WITH FRENCH TO KIMBERLEY

The Boers were down on Kimberley with siege and
    Maxim gun;
The Boers were down on Kimberley, their numbers
    ten to one!
Faint were the hopes the British had to make the
    struggle good—
Defenceless in an open plain the Diamond City stood.
They built them forts with bags of sand, they fought
    from roof and wall,
They flashed a message to the south, 'Help! or the
    town must fall!'

Then down our ranks the order ran to march at
dawn of day,
And French was off to Kimberley to drive the Boers
away.

He made no march along the line; he made no front
attack
Upon those Magersfontein heights that held the
Seaforths back;
But eastward over pathless plains, by open veldt and
vley,
Across the front of Cronje's force his troopers held
their way.
The springbuck, feeding on the flats where Modder
River runs,
Were startled by his horses' hoofs, the rumble of his
guns.
The Dutchman's spies that watched his march from
every rocky wall
Rode back in haste: 'He marches East! He threatens
Jacobsdal!'
Then north he wheeled as wheels the hawk, and
showed to their dismay.
That French was off to Kimberley to drive the Boers
away.

His column was five thousand strong—all mounted
men—and guns:
There met, beneath the world-wide flag, the world-
wide Empire's sons;
They came to prove to all the earth that kinship
conquers space,
And those who fight the British Isles must fight the
British race!
From far New Zealand's flax and fern, from cold
Canadian snows,
From Queensland plains, where hot as fire the
summer sunshine glows—

And in the front the Lancers rode that New South
    Wales had sent:
With easy stride across the plain their long, lean
    Walers went.
Unknown, untried, those squadrons were, but proudly
    out they drew
Beside the English regiments that fought at
    Waterloo.
From every coast, from every clime, they met in
    proud array
To go with French to Kimberley to drive the Boers
    away.

He crossed the Reit and fought his way towards the
    Modder bank.
The foeman closed behind his march, and hung upon
    the flank.
The long, dry grass was all ablaze (and fierce the
    veldt fire runs);
He fought them through a wall of flame that blazed
    around the guns!
Then limbered up and drove at speed, though horses
    fell and died;
We might not halt for man nor beast on that wild,
    daring ride.
Black with the smoke and parched with thirst, we
    pressed the livelong day
Our headlong march to Kimberley to drive the Boers
    away.

We reached the drift at fall of night, and camped
    across the ford.
Next day from all the hills around the Dutchman's
    cannon roared.

A narrow pass ran through the hills, with guns on
     either side;
The boldest man might well turn pale before that
     pass he tried,
For, if the first attack should fail, then every hope
     was gone:
But French looked once, and only once, and then he
     said, 'Push on!'
The gunners plied their guns amain; the hail of
     shrapnel flew;
With rifle fire and lancer charge their squadrons
     back we threw;
And through the pass between the hills we swept in
     furious fray,
And French was through to Kimberley to drive the
     Boers away.

First published in the *Sydney
Morning Herald*, 29 September
1900. This version appeared in
Rio Grande's Last Race, 1902.

JOHNNY BOER

Men fight all shapes and sizes as the racing horses
     run,
And no man knows his courage till he stands before
     a gun.
At mixed-up fighting, hand to hand, and clawing men
     about
They reckon Fuzzy-Wuzzy is the hottest fighter out.
But Fuzzy gives himself away—his style is out of date,
He charges like a driven grouse that rushes on its
     fate;

You've nothing in the world to do but pump him full
　　of lead:
But when you're fighting Johnnie Boer you have to
　　use your head;
He don't believe in front attacks or charging at the
　　run,
He fights you from a kopje with his little Maxim
　　gun.

For when the Lord He made the earth, it seems
　　uncommon clear,
He gave the job of Africa to some good engineer,
Who started building fortresses on fashions of his
　　own—
Lunettes, redoubts, and counterscarps all made of
　　rock and stone.
The Boer needs only bring a gun, for ready to his
　　hand
He finds these heaven-built fortresses all scattered
　　through the land;
And there he sits and winks his eye and wheels his
　　gun about,
And we must charge across the plain to hunt the
　　beggar out.
It ain't a game that grows on us—there's lots of
　　better fun
Than charging at old Johnny with his little Maxim
　　gun.

On rocks a goat could scarcely climb, steep as the
　　walls of Troy,
He wheels a four-point-seven about as easy as a
　　toy;
With bullocks yoked and drag-ropes manned, he
　　lifts her up the rocks
And shifts her every now and then, as cunning as a
　　fox.

At night you mark her right ahead, you see her clean
    and clear,
Next day at dawn—'What, ho! she bumps'—from
    somewhere in the rear.
Or else the keenest-eyed patrol will miss him with
    the glass—
He's lying hidden in the rocks to let the leaders pass;
But when the mainguard comes along he opens up
    the fun;
There's lots of ammunition for the little Maxim gun.

But after all the job is sure, although the job is slow,
We have to see the business through, the Boer has
    got to go.
With Nordenfeldt and lyddite shell it's certain, soon
    or late,
We'll hunt him from his kopjes and across the
    Orange State;
And then across those open flats you'll see the beggar
    run,
And we'll be running after with *our* little Maxim gun.

> First published in the *Sydney Mail*,
> 17 February 1900. This version
> appeared in *Rio Grande's Last
> Race*, 1902.

From the Boer Side

Interview with Olive Schreiner

ARUNDEL *Jan 21*
'Our friend the enemy!' For six weeks the New South
Wales Lancers (with whom the present scribe is associated
as war correspondent) had been in daily touch with the
Boers. Six weeks of blazing hot days and freezing cold

nights, spent in tents where the dust storms coated everything with a dull-red powder, out on picket duty lying in the scorching sun among the rocks of a kopje, or on patrol trying how near we could get to the enemy without being shot dead; six weeks of hurried movements, of midnight marches and rapid shiftings of camp, of night-long watches out in the cold of the veldt with the shivering horses standing alongside; and all with the object of killing, capturing, or dispersing the unknown and practically unseen enemy that clung so tenaciously to his heaven-built fortress of rocky kopje, and who was so ready to shoot on the slightest provocation. We had given up thinking what the Boers were like or of considering them as human beings at all. To us they were simply so much enemy—as impersonal as the Maxim guns and the rifles that they used. For six weeks we had seen no letters, no books, and practically no newspapers. The world was narrowed down to ourselves and the enemy. All our time was fully occupied in fighting, and we gave no thought to the question of what the fighting was about. It was a great change, therefore, in visiting Capetown to call on Olive Schreiner, a bitter opponent of the war, and to hear the Boer side of the question.

The authoress of *The Story of an African Farm* needs no introduction to Australians. Born in South Africa and reared among the farmers, she is an Afrikander, of the Afrikanders; and while her brother (the Premier of the Cape Colony) has been very reserved in expressing opinions, Olive Schreiner has been most outspoken in denouncing the war and those who, in her opinion, are responsible for it. She lives at Newlands, a suburb of Cape Town, and no Australian city has such a suburb. On leaving the train one walks down an avenue overhung with splendid trees, and more like a private carriageway than a public road. It is hard to believe that one is not trespassing on somebody's private garden. There is no sidewalk—just the red-earth avenue between the trees. The flowers and trees grow most luxuriantly, sunflowers, box-hedges, roses, and all manner of grasses flourishing everywhere, an inexpressible relief after the miles of sunburnt karoo desert we have been staring over lately. The houses that front on the avenue all stand back in their own gardens but instead of having a forbidding six-foot paling fence round each property, there is usually a low iron-standard fence or a box-hedge as boundary, and the passer-by sees into these beautiful gardens as he goes along. If a few residences were erected in Sydney Botanic Gardens that would be like Newlands. The trees are just as beautiful and luxuriant. In these surroundings lives the woman who made her name famous by *The Story of an African Farm*. She is married now, but still prefers to be known as Olive Schreiner. She is a little woman, small in stature, but of very strong physique, broad and powerful; her face olive-complexioned, with bright restless eyes and a quick mobile mouth.

She talks fluently, and with tremendous energy, and one is not long in arriving at the conclusion that she is thoroughly in earnest—deadly earnest—over this question of the Boer war. It may be news to many Australians to hear that in the Cape Colony there are more people against the war than for it, not necessarily Boer sympathisers, but people who think that the war should never have been entered upon. When our troops landed from Australia, we were astonished to find that the Cape Colony was so much against the war. The local papers that were for the war were all clamouring for the arrest or dismissal of Schreiner, the Premier, but when the House went to a division, Schreiner had a majority behind him, and Schreiner has always declared that England is not justified in this war. Olive Schreiner was not long in stating her views to the present writer. She talks rapidly and energetically, emphasising her remarks with uplifted flavour. 'You Australians and New Zealanders and Canadians,' she said, 'I cannot understand it at all, why you come here light-heartedly to shoot down other colonists of whom you know nothing—it is terrible. Such fine men too—fine fellows. I went to Green Point, and saw your men in camp; Oh, they were fine men—(these were Colonel Williams's A.M.C. troops)—and to think that they are going out to kill and be killed, just to please the capitalists! There was one officer—Oh a fine man, so like a Boer, he might have been a Boer commandant. It is terrible—such men to come and fight against those fighting for their liberty and their country. The English Tommy Atkins goes where he is sent—he fights because he is ordered; but you people—you are all volunteers! Why have you come? ... You say that England was at war, and you wished to show the world that when the mother country got into war the colonies were prepared to take their place beside her! Yes, but you ought to ask, you ought to make inquiries before you come over. You Australians do not understand. This is a capitalists' war! They want to get control of the Rand and the mines. You have nothing like it in your country. You have a working class that votes and that cannot be brought to vote against its own interests; but in the Transvaal there are just a handful of Boer farmers, a small but enormously wealthy mine-owning class and their dependants—professional men, shopkeepers, and so on, and the rest are all Kaffirs.'

'Why didn't the Boers grant the franchise?'

'It was not really wanted. I was in Johannesburg a few months before the war broke out, and hundreds of men there said that they would not forgo their British nationality for the sake of voting as a Boer. They were all nomads, wanderers, over there to make money, and if Oom Paul had gone on his knees and asked them to accept the franchise they would not have accepted it.

They would not relinquish being British subjects. But the capitalists insist on getting hold of the mines, and all the white people are so concerned with them, their interests so depend on the mine owners, that they must go along with them, and now they want the franchise to take control of the mines from the Boers. It is a monstrous war, and England will regret it; it is just to take the country from the Boers for the benefit of the speculators. For years this war has been worked up—all sorts of stories have been printed of the Boers and their ignorance and their savagery. They are all lies. I was a governess among the Boers for years, and no kinder people exist. They are clever too. Young Boers go to England and succeed at the Universities; they become doctors and lawyers and politicians. It is much like Australia from what I have read. They are such hospitable people.

'Oh, this war is a terrible thing; it will be a war of extermination. What do you think will be the end of it? There will be no end. The Boers are fighting for life or death, and they have no idea of giving in. If they are beaten back into the Free State and the Transvaal that is just the time they will be most dangerous. When the English get to Pretoria with their army they will then be in a worse position than they are now. They will have hundreds and hundreds of miles of railway lines to defend, and even if the Boers are scattered and beaten they will still fight. The Boer women now are heart and soul for the war. The Boer farmer is a curious man. He marries early, usually about 18 or 19, and there is not one man in the army against you but has his wife and child somewhere. And those wives and children are reaping the crops and working the farms, so that their husbands can go to the war. After Elandslaagte, where the Boers were defeated, one Boer went home. His wife said, "What has happened; are you wounded?" "No." "Is the enemy fled?" "No." "Well, back you go to the laager, and fight with the rest." Another old man of 75, when he heard of the defeat, rose up and took his rifle. "I am going to the front," he said. "Why, you cannot see," said his grandchildren. "I cannot see at 1000 yards," he said, "but I can see well enough at 100"; and off he went in a Cape cart as he was too old to ride. The small boys at school at the Cape Town schools have all been brought back to the farms to fight—boys of 14 and 15 are in the ranks. And all of these people have their relatives all through Cape Colony; and they are to be butchered, and the English soldiers are to be butchered, to suit a few capitalists. It will benefit no one else. The effect of this war on South Africa will be everlasting; we have such a large population here who feel that the war is unjust, and they will never forgive the English people for forcing it on. Perhaps the memory of Majuba Hill had a good deal to do with it? I cannot think so—the English are not so narrow as to treasure memories of a small thing like that. But now it is a long, terrible war that is before us, and the Boers will be more dangerous after a few reverses. A few defeats will not crush them! When the English get to Pretoria then there will begin the trouble.'

Whatever maybe the correctness of Olive Schreiner's views, there is no doubt of her sincerity. She says openly what most, or at any rate very many, South Africans think, and it is always well to hear both sides, so I have put down without comment exactly what her views were.

Taking on literary matters, Olive Schreiner said that though she was constantly writing she did not publish much. The cares of household life interfered much with work. When a governess in the Transvaal, after the day's work was done, she would sit in her room and work with a mind free from care. It was then that *The African Farm* was written. Nowadays she has too much to think about— household worries, and so on. She was asked to act as war correspondent for a New York paper, but the authorities would not hear of her going—in which, by the way, they were quite right. The front is no place for a woman.

It seems a pity that this woman, who is no doubt a great literary genius, should be wasting her time and wearing out her energies over this Boer war question, instead of giving us another book as good as her first one; but after an interview with her one comes away with a much more lively and human interest in 'our friends the enemy'. If things are as she says, if the Boers are going to make it a war to the bitter end, then England has a sorry task before her. If the Boers scatter and break to the mountains they will be practically unreachable, and the English people are too humane to care about levying reprisals by destroying their homesteads and leaving their wives and children without shelter. The result will be that even after the war is over a large force will have to be kept in the country to maintain order, and with the Cape disaffected there will be serious trouble for politicians after the soldiers have got through with their work. One is more inclined to hope that after a defeat or two the Boer, sensible man that he is, will come in under English rule and rely on the forbearance of that Power rather than maintain a hopeless struggling fight which will only prolong the misery of the present war.

Sydney Morning Herald, 17 February 1900

AT THE FRONT

BLOEMFONTEIN, *March 25*
We are still outside this place, camped on the side of a big green hill, with a maize and melon field alongside,

and we have nothing to do but try to cure our horses' backs and ride into the town buying clothes and listening to the absurd rumours that always spring up in a camp after a day or two's idleness. No one knew for some days where Buller's force had got to, and it was reported to be in Johannesburg, in Pretoria, and in fact in all sorts of impossible places. Then at last a man came in from Buller and said that the latter had not left Ladysmith; consequently, when we heard that four officers of the Guards had been sent in wounded by the Boers, we thought it was another camp lie, but it turned out to be true.

Personality of Kipling

While in town inquiring into a certain matter I had the luck to meet Kipling. He has come up here on a hurried visit, and partly in search of health after his late severe illness. He is a little, squat-figured, sturdy man of about 40. His face is well enough known to everybody from his numerous portraits, but no portrait gives any hint of the quick nervous energy of the man. His talk is a gabble, a chatter, a constant jumping from one point to another, and he seizes the chief idea in each subject unerringly. In manner he is more like a business man than a literary celebrity. There is nothing of the dreamer about him, and the last thing one could believe was that the little square-figured man with the thick black eyebrows and the round glasses was the creator of Mowgli the jungle-boy, of 'The Drums of the Fore-and-aft' and of *The Man Who Would be King*, to say nothing of Ortheris, Mulvaney, and Learoyd, and a host of others. He talked of little but the war and its results, present and prospective. His residence in America has Americanised his language and he says 'yep', instead of 'yes'. After talking for some time about Australian books and Australian papers he launched out on what is evidently his ruling idea at present—the future of South Africa. 'I'm off back to London,' he said, 'booked to sail on the 11th. I'm not going to wait for the fighting here. I can trust the army to do all the fighting here. It's in London I'll have to do my fighting. I want to fight the people who will say, "The Boers fought for freedom—give them back their country!" I want to fight all that sort of nonsense. I know all about it. I knew the war was coming, and I came over here some time ago and went to Johannesburg and Pretoria, and I've got everything good and ready. There's going to be the greatest demand for skilled labour here the world has ever known. Railways, irrigation, mines, mills, all would have started years ago only for this Government.'

I asked what sort of Government he proposed to put in place of the Boers'.

'Military rule for three years, and by that time they will have enough population here to govern themselves. We want you Australians to stay over here and help fetch this place along.'

I said that our men did not think the country worth fighting over, and that all we had seen would not pay to farm, unless one were sure of water.

'Water! You can get artesian water at 40 feet anywhere! What more do they want?'

I pointed out that there is a vast difference between artesian water which rises to the surface, and well water which has to be lifted 40 feet. When it comes to watering 100 000 sheep, one finds the difference.

'Oh well,' he said, 'I don't know about that; but anyhow, you haven't seen the best of the country. You've only seen 500 miles of karoo desert yet. Wait till you get to the Transvaal!'

'Will there be much more fighting, do you think?'

'Well, there's sure to be some more, and the soldiers want to get their money back.'

'How do you mean, get their money back?'

'Get some revenge out of the Boers for the men we've lost—get our money back. The Tommies don't count the lot captured with Cronje at all. They're all alive, and our men are dead. We want to get some of our money back. You Australians have fought well,' he went on, 'very well. Real good men. Now we want you to stay here and help us along with this show. I can't understand there being so many radicals in Australia. What do they want? If they were to become independent, what do they expect to do? Will they fork out the money for a fleet and a standing army? They'd be a dead gift to Germany if they didn't. What more do they want than what they've got?'

I didn't feel equal to enlightening him on Australian politics, so I said, 'What are you going to do with the Boers if you take their country?'

'Let 'em stop on their farms.'

'Won't they vote against you as soon as you give them the votes back? Won't they revert to their old order of things?'

'Not a bit. We'll have enough people to outvote 'em before we give 'em the votes. There'll be no Irish question here. Once they find they're under a Government that don't commandeer everything they've got, they'll settle down and work all right. They're working away now to the north of us, entrenching away like beavers; we'll give them something better to do than digging trenches.'

One could almost see the man's mind working while he talked, and yet all the time while he was talking with quick nervous utterance of the great things to be done in those unsettled countries I seemed to see behind him the heavy impassive face of the man I saw in Kimberley— Cecil Rhodes. Kipling is the man of thought and speech, Rhodes the man of action. Cecil Rhodes seems to own most things in these parts, and when our Australians reach the promised land of which Kipling speaks so enthusiastically, they will be apt to find the best claims already staked out by Cecil Rhodes and his fellow-investors, at least that is my impression. There are no fortunes 'going spare' in this part of the world; but anyhow this is not a political letter, and Kipling is big enough to draw his own rations, and if he chooses to temporarily lay aside the pen of the author for the carpet bag of the politicians, it is his own lookout. He expressed great interest in the Australian horses, and promised to come out to the camp and see them, and he gave us a graphic account of the way in which an Australian buckjumper had got rid of him in India. 'I seemed to be sitting on great eternal chaos,' he said, 'and then the world slipped away from under me, and that's all I remember.'

He looks pale and sallow after his illness, but seems a strong man, one that will live many years if his brain doesn't wear his body out.

Australian Troops

Let us return now to our muttons, or at any rate our Australians. I rode over and saw Colonel Knight's men and horses yesterday. Captain Antill's men are attacked to Knight's command now. Antill's troop have been a long time here, and have settled down, and their saddles are fairly good, so that the whole force are fit for action; but Colonel Knight's men were sent from Australia with saddles I wouldn't put on a mule, and many of the horses are dying, weakened by hard work, under-feeding, colds and sore backs. The question of saddles and sore backs is the great cavalry question from one generation to another. Books have been written on it, speeches made about it, kingdoms have risen and fallen on the question of cavalry saddles; and the thing is as far from a settlement as ever. It isn't the bullet of the foe that the cavalry has to fear, it is the sore-backed horse that cripples the regiment, and leaves hundreds of men on foot useless.

The Australian and the Boer

While I am writing this in Bloemfontein Club, most of the original members of that club are digging trenches around Kroonstad, and it is freely rumoured that they are holding a Volksraad there to decide whether they shall fight on or not. We don't care how soon they surrender, we are not like Kipling's soldiers, wanting any 'money back'. And talking of 'money back', I may as well close with a little incident, in which an Australian and a Boer figured as follows:

When Cronje surrendered, and his men came bundling out of the trenches, each man with a carpet bag in one hand, and a rifle in the other, a great many of them were leading horses laden with all their goods and chattels. One burgher had a very fine, creamy pony, and on this animal he had at least a hundredweight of luggage of various sorts, rugs, blankets, a sugar bag, a carpet bag, some boots, and innumerable other things. One of our Lancer officers took a fancy to the pony, and offered the Boer £1 for him. As he was sure to lose the pony as soon as he became a prisoner he was willing enough to take the pound. But the trouble was—how was he to shift his luggage? He was solemnly assured that Lord Roberts would be certain to send a cart for his luggage, and on this idea he took the sovereign, unloaded the pony, and handed him over, and sat down cheerfully smoking beside his pile of luggage. He had hardly got comfortably seated when a Tommy came up with a fixed bayonet and said, 'Now, then, move off your hank! Don't you see the others movin' off! Come along! Where's the—what? The cart for your luggage? Leave it 'ere, mate, leave it 'ere and I'll tell Lord Kitchener about it.' By dint of dividing it up among his friends, he got it along somehow, and the pony, with an English shrapnel bullet in his jaw is now an officer's servant's charger, and a very good little animal he is.

We expect to move north in ten days. The corps from

New South Wales has been given charge of the main hospital building here, and is doing great work. Majors Scot-Skirving and MacCormick are just in time for plenty of hard work. We have no tents, and the weather is getting bitterly cold at night. Curiously enough, we are probably the only English-speaking people that have never heard 'The Absent-Minded Beggar'* sung or recited. When we get back, and hear the tune, we will wonder what it is. The English papers are full of 'Absent-Minded Beggar' concerts. Probably you are just as full of it . . .

Sydney Morning Herald, 12 May 1900

* Kipling's piece of quickie verse on the Boer War, which had captured patriotic imagination.

A Day Under Fire:
A Battlefield Sketch

It is grey dawn. The stars are growing pale in the cold frosty sky, and away to the east a faint, cheerless white light begins to spread over the plain. Away on all sides spreads the dimly seen stretch of veldt, in some places reaching to the limit of human sight, in others terminating abruptly in some towering rocky mound called a kopje. Hidden in under the shelter of one of these kopjes lies a military camp, the only signs of life being rows and rows of horses tied by the heads to picket-pegs. With drooping heads they stand half asleep, each horse facing his saddle, which is laid upon the ground in front of him. Against each saddle is what appears to be a small roll of blankets, but which is in reality the sleeping form of a soldier. A deathlike stillness reigns over everything. Behind the rows of horses are a few cannons with the horses tied to ropes stretched from gun to gun, and behind these again are transport wagons and ambulances, with the mules tied in groups beside each vehicle. In front of the rows of horses are a few shabby old two-wheeled carts, piled with luggage and cooking things. These are the officers' mess carts, and all round them lie the blanket-shrouded forms of the mess cooks and officers' servants. Under each cart is an officer's sleeping valise, a canvas affair laid on the ground, and in this the occupant lies placidly sleeping. The rows of horses are divided off into three sections, each section being a separate regiment, and the three regiments together forming a brigade. At one of the sections a small forest of lances, stuck upright in the ground, indicates a Lancer Regiment; the others are Dragoons or Hussars. The weary, half-starved horses, the worn saddles, and the recumbent men, make a picture as different as possible from the accepted idea of a cavalry camp; but for all that these are some of French's dashing cavalry, the men who by relieving Kimberley changed the whole aspect of the Boer war.

As the light grows more definite a ghostly figure flits about in each regimental camp rousing the sleepers. To some he applies his foot with no light force. He is the sergeant-major—the man on whose shoulders the whole of the hard work falls; the man who is the buffer between the officers and the men. 'Turn out, lads! Turn out!' he says. 'Do you want to be there till you get sun struck?' (N.B.—The sun is as yet only indicated by a pale glow on the horizon.)

To hear his tones one would imagine him the greatest bully in the world. The men sit up as he passes along, and uncoil themselves out of their blankets. They have all gone to bed in their boots and clothes, so their toilet simply consists in rubbing their eyes. As he pushes one bundle of blankets with his foot a muffled groan rises from the occupant. At once the sergeant's tone changes. 'Who's this?' he says. 'Oh, it's you, Charley. Don't you feel any better?'

'I'm pretty seedy, major' (abbreviation of 'sergeant-major'), and the man rolls to a sitting position, showing a ghastly white face, and feverish eyes staring over a stubbly unshaven beard. 'Why don't you go sick? Come on sick parade this morning.'

'No, I'd go in. Ask Billy to saddle my horse. I'll be up in a minute,' and the man sinks down again and tosses uneasily as the sergeant passes on. By this time the whole camp is astir, the cooks are bending over huge cooking pots, nosebags are put on the horses, and a steady sound of crunching grain rises from the 500 or so horses all eating at once. The officers upheave themselves from under their carts and shave hurriedly, and eat their breakfast in silence, shivering with cold.

Just as the sun shows above the horizon an order comes along the line, and is repeated by each squadron leader, 'Stand to your horses!' It comes down from squadron to squadron. 'Stand to your horses!' And the men gulp down the last morsels of their breakfasts and run to their horses' heads, and the ranks close up. 'Prepare to mount!' comes along from squadron to squadron; and then, 'Mount!' and the whole brigade are on horseback. 'By column of troops from the right, walk, march!' is the next order, and the advance squadron rides off, followed at intervals by the main body, with the guns clanking along in the centre. The brigade is making a flank attack to act conjointly with a centre attack made by infantry some five miles away on their right. The infantry won't move for some hour or two yet, as the cavalry have to push on ahead and get round the end of the line of hills, which are towering to the sky some seven or eight miles ahead; so off the cavalry go, riding leisurely through the long dewy grass, the men smoking and yarning together, utterly careless of the fact that they are to be under fire in a few hours. Behind the fighting columns comes a long string of transport wagons, ambulances, and mess carts, reaching over a couple of miles of ground. And thus at walking pace, like some enormous funeral, the brigade moves on across the open veldt. Before one has time to notice it the advance squadron has thrown out reconnoitring parties, and a sort of screen of men is spread out across the veldt, a mile or two in front of the brigade, the men riding just within hearing of each other.

Suddenly those in the rear hear a faint sound away in the front, a sort of rattling sound, as if a cart with a loose wheel were being driven along the hillside. Clack-clack, clack-clack, it goes, and at once the men far away in the advance wheel their horses and come dashing back to the main body, while the little puffs of dust rising in the plain show where the bullets are landing. They have located the enemy, and the next question is are we to go round the hill or attack it. Ever since the Magersfontein disaster no general cares to make a direct front attack on a position if it can be avoided. So the long serpentine column coils itself away to the left like a cautious boa-constrictor, leaving a small force to watch the hill and prevent any attack from it. A mile or two is covered and the flank of the hill is turned, bringing a lot of new country into view and revealing a low, scrub-covered kopje right in front and a huge hill towering up on the left. Almost as soon as these come into view a number of mounted men are seen coming from behind the low kopje and making for the big hill. In the distance they look like toys as they scuttle across to the hill, but, great as the distance is, modern gunnery laughs at it.

General French is at the head of his column, and he gives a sharp message to a galloper riding by him—'Bring up the guns at once.' The cavalry open out and through the gap the guns come up at a gallop. There are many fine sights in the world, but it is the sight of a lifetime to see the Royal Horse Artillery gallop into action. With a rush and a clatter and a swing the guns fly past behind the madly straining horses, while the drivers ply their whips, and the men on the limbers with clenched teeth hold to their seats as the guns rock and sway with the pace they are making. 'Action front,' and round come the trained horses like machinery, and like lightning the men uncouple the limber and place the gun in position. The range is calculated and the order goes: 'At three thousand. Fuse fourteen. Ready. Fire number one gun!' and with an exulting scream, like a living thing released from prison, away goes the shell across to the little knot of galloping men. An absolute silence prevails as the shell whizzes away out of hearing, and then 'bang!' It has burst right over the little dust cloud that is travelling across the plain. It is a splendid shot, and a buzz of congratulation arises, and a wild feeling of exultation wakes in every man's breast.

This is something like sport, this shooting of human game with cannon over three thousand yards of country. 'Hooray! Give 'em another!' The second gun fires, and the shell whizzes away, and the same dead silence reigns, when suddenly another note is struck—a discordant note this time. From the rocky tree-covered hill in the direct front, only half a mile off, comes a clear tock-tock, tock-tock—a couple of clear double reports, and something seems to whistle by the gunners, making a noise like a heavy wind blowing through a very small crack in the door. Pee-u-u-u-w. It is the thinnest, shrillest sound, this whistle of a bullet at short range. Most of the men duck instinctively as the first bullet goes over. Pee-u-u-u-w! Pee-u-u-u-w! They come by thick enough now, and each man's heart sinks as he sees what the column is let in for. Here we have marched all the guns and horses, without cover, to within half a mile of a hill, and the Boers have seized it while we were shooting at their mounted men! Pee-u-u-u-w! Pee-u-u-u-w! That fellow was close!

The General sees the trouble at once. 'Dismount, all you men with carbines! Get the horses back. Keep the guns working!' And he and his staff turn away as the men jump off their horses and run up to the front and lie down in a long row, from which a rippling, rattling fire soon breaks out. The horses are taken back, and the guns and the dismounted men are left alone for a duel to the death with the foe in the hill. Now is the time to see the Royal Horse Artillery at its best! All the years of training, all the hard toil of drilling and practising reap their reward here now. The men serve the guns with machine-like precision; the battery-major, with his hands behind his back, stalks up and down behind his guns exactly as a gamecock stalks about his barnyard; there is defiance in every motion as he marches quickly from gun to gun, watching where the shells are landing, and giving quick directions as he passes. The R.H.A. will 'take on' any living kind of gun that will stand up to them within their range. To go into action under heavy rifle fire at 800 yards is suicide according to the drill books, but here they do it with a light heart. 'Shoot, and be——' is the motto of the R.H.A. 'Let us see who will get sick of it first!' And they send the shells, as fast as ever the guns can be worked, whizzing into the hill, where the steady tock-tock, tock-tock still keeps up, and they never flinch, though the hurried white-faced stretcher bearers run up and carry man after man wounded to the rear.

A Personal View

And now, having introduced the *dramatis personae*, let us take a personal view of what it feels like to be under fire under such conditions as above described. The reader must imagine that he has ridden up behind the guns just before the rifles opened on them. These are his thoughts and sensations:

Hurrah! Look at the Boers scooting. Give 'em another round. That's a good shell! Pee-u-u-u-w, pee-u-u-u-w, pee-u-u-u-w. Great heavens, they've got that hill in front of us. That's just like French, always going bull-headed into

these sort of places. Pee-u-u-u-w. You duck instinctively.
A man on French's staff turns and says, 'Let us get back.
No sense staying here!' You turn with him, and walk a
few paces, leading the horses. Pee-u-u-u-w. Pee-u-u-u-w.
The dust kicks up in front, and a few twigs fall from a
tree overhead. Crack! Your companion staggers forward,
and you catch him before he falls. 'Have you got it?' 'Yes,'
he gasps, 'I'm done for. Hit through the body!' A doctor
is hurrying past, and you hail him sharply. 'Here! Here's
a man badly hit.' You pick him up between you, and
carry him back, and all the time the bullets whistle past,
and the wounded man almost shrieks with pain. 'Put
him down here,' says the doctor, selecting the base of a
small bush, and carefully you lay the sufferer down. The
doctor makes a hasty examination, and silently puts a
bandage round the body. 'How bad is it?' mutters the
wounded man. 'Is it through the body?' 'Not at all, not at
all,' says the medico, 'only through the loins. You'll be all
right.' He lies glibly but unconvincingly, and the sufferer's
face grows an ashen grey. The doctor hurries off, and you
are left along with the dying man.

It is an unenviable experience. He talks in a feeble
voice about his wife—always about his wife! 'I wouldn't
care so much if it wasn't for my wife!' You try to cheer
him with well-meant falsehoods, such as saying, 'You'll
be all right in no time'—mere sound and fury signifying
nothing. Meanwhile the guns just in front roar away,
and from your lair in the grass you can see the battery-
major stalking grimly up and down. Pee-u-u-u-w, pee-
u-u-u-w, they still whistle over. A horse comes and stands
by the tree—a loose horse who has got away from his
rider. Whack! He has got it through the body, and that
horse will carry a rider no more. It is awful how hard a
bullet hits. One would imagine from the small hole it
makes that it caused little shock. But it hits like a sledge-
hammer—a terrific blow. The wretched horse staggers
away to die, and you lie very flat beside the still man
and peer through the grass at the battery-major, still

stalking by his guns. We have got a Maxim into action now and a pom-pom gun, and the clatter and noise are something hellish. Surely that must drive the Boers back, but in every lull of the firing there comes the steady tock-tock, tock-tock from away in the hill. Why does the Mauser make a double report? you wonder vaguely, but the more pressing question is 'Will our guns be able to drive them back?' Whir-r-rp! A bullet buries itself in the sand alongside you—a nasty, vicious sound it is too, and the sick man winces slightly at the sound. 'They'll take our guns,' he says, 'and then come and take us.' 'Not a bit,' you say, but you feel that he is probably about right. Far away on a hill you can see the horses of a cavalry regiment, who have dismounted, and are trying to advance on the Boers under cover. The rattle of their carbines comes faintly from among the rocks. Suddenly a couple of men rush up and deposit a wounded Tommy beside you, and leave him without a word. They think you are a doctor. He is hit through the knee, but makes no complaint. There is no such stoic as the Tommy. A Chinaman is an hysterical being compared to him.

Now the Boers have got a pom-pom onto us, and the shells fly screaming over like a flight of evil birds. Luckily they are all aimed at someone far in the rear. 'Is that the Boers' pom-pom?' says the sick man. 'Yes.' 'Why don't our dismounted men go?' he mutters. You think the same thing—the advance of the mounted men seems painfully slow when you are under fire yourself. 'What ridgment is it, sir?' says the Tommy. 'The Seven D.G.'s,' you reply (Seventh Dragoon Guards). 'Ah! That's a good ridgment— the Black Seventh,' says the Tommy, and relapses into stoical silence again. Not a word about his own wounds, because the man beside him is an officer, and it is almost a presumption for a Tommy to be wounded alongside an officer. Now, surely the Boer fire is dying down. For a while they haven't fired a shot, and the deafening clatter of our guns is kept up incessantly. Then comes a pause, a lull, and then again the accursed tock-tock, tock-tock, and a whole rattle breaks out, and the bullets whistle incessantly over, and you bury your nose in the ground, and lie as flat as you can. The sick man says, 'I thought so. They'll take the guns.' It seems our guns are silent for want of ammunition, and a man rushes past, his arms full of cartridges. He pauses by the tree a second, and delivers himself of this remarkable speech, addressed to the universe in general, 'All I have to say is—the ammunition bearer is a—hero!' He is so excited he doesn't know what he is saying. Another man comes past, a skulker, keeping back out of the firing line. He affects great interest in the wounded officer. 'Is he very bad, sir,' he says. 'Clear away out of this; don't bring the fire on us,' is the answer he gets, and then pee-u-u-u-w, a bullet whizzes past within an inch of his head. He ducks hurriedly, and scuttles off without a word. Then comes the boom of a far-off gun, and buz-z-z comes the shell, getting louder and finally passing over—the embodiment of destructiveness. You reflect what a frightful thing war is. 'God save Australia from war for ever and ever!'

Suddenly from the far hill you hear the boom, boom, boom, of many guns, and your heart leaps. The other brigade has got round and taken them in flank and they must retire now. The tock-tock dies away, and you rise from the grass, and catch a glimpse of a few mounted figures dashing across the open to the shelter of some hills. A few men are lying in odd positions near the guns—don't look at them too closely, they are dead men. The battery-major still walks up and down with his defiant strut. You wonder how he has stood it all through the firing. The ambulance comes and takes off the wounded officer and the wounded Tommy, and you go back to the bivouac quite overstrained and nerveless—you have had a morning under fire.

FROM: THE PURSUIT OF DE WET

... Coming along on this march we have had white frosts
every night; the thermometer stood at 18 this morning
in our camp. The country is very monotonous, and one
camp is much like another. The farmers are mostly
back on their farms. We never can get hold of those
farmers' names properly, and every third farm is named
Rietfontein, so we invent our own names for the places
as we go along; we called one very cold camp Snowy
River, another (where the supply wagons didn't come
up) was Poverty Flat, and so on; and we called every
dutchman Mr. Hoopenjabber. Nine times out of ten it is
so like their own name that they don't know the differ-
ence. The procedure on arrival at each farm is always
the same. Rimington's scouts as a rule get to the farms
first, and as they all speak Dutch they have a yarn with
Hoopenjabber, get any fresh eggs and butter that there
may be in the house, and have a drink of coffee and ride
off, and Hoopenjabber thinks the British army are not
half so bad, and is quite bending when the General and
his staff ride up. Then his troubles commence. The D.M.I.
(Director of Military Intelligence) sends for him, and starts
to interrogate him. Now, the D.M.I. is invariably a staff
officer, who knows nothing about Africa or the Dutch,
and his only ideas of getting information is to ask
questions in a loud voice, which at once frightens the
Dutchman into shamming ignorance. The Dutchman's
wife and an interpreter are always present, and a dia-
logue like this generally follows:

Staff Officer (in a loud threatening voice): 'What's your
name?'

Dutchman (cringingly, after hurried consultation with
his wife): 'Cornelius Hoopenjabber.'

'What's the name of this farm?'

'Rietfontein.'

'But the last farm was called Rietfontein. This can't be Rietfontein.'

Long and animated discussion between the Dutchman and his wife and the interpreter, which ends in chaos, and the name of the farm remains a mystery.

Staff Officer: 'Ask him when he was with the commando last.'

More jabber, resulting in the following:

'He says he wasn't in the commando at all; his wife was sick, so they didn't commandeer him.'

'Ask him are there any Boers near here, and ask him where his rifle is.'

At this Hoopenjabber forgets his assumed ignorance of the English language and becomes fluent. He says: 'De Boers have all trek. I gave my rifle to de officer' (meaning the Remington Scout), and he produces a receipt for the rifle, which is scrutinised and passed as correct. Then his features work convulsively, and at last he gasps out, 'Can I have a pass—?' And the D.M.I., having acquired all the above useless knowledge, gives him a pass, with which he probably goes back to the commando. This farce goes on at each farm, and the amount of ignorance that the D.M.I. accumulates is something extraordinary ...

Sydney Morning Herald, 21 August 1900

AN INFORMAL LETTER FROM LONDON

A Yellow Gloom

I arrived in London on the evening of the record fog; this whole city was choking in a kind of yellow gloom, out of which the whistles of the bus conductors and the shouts of cabmen rose like the din of fiends in a pit of torment. The theatres nearly all closed their doors. Trafalgar

Square was full of buses all night; buses that had failed to make their way home, and simply pulled up and waited for daylight, with their passengers huddled inside; the cabmen wouldn't even try to take people home—a five-pound note was vainly offered by one man for a drive of half an hour—what would have been half an hour's drive if there had been any light, or even any decent sort of darkness to drive by; but this awful yellow shroud choked everything; and yet, talking it over with an English bus driver next morning he said with the greatest pride, 'Ah! You don't see fogs like that in no other part of the world!' There is a beautiful serene self-complacency about these people that one can never sufficiently admire. We were moving up the Strand in a stream of traffic, doing about four miles an hour, halted every now and again by policemen, the old well-trained bus horses picking their way along like two well-regulated machines; and the busman said to me with conscious superiority, 'Ah! You don't see drivin' like this in no other part of the world!' I thought of various little bits of driving that I had seen some of Cobb and Co.'s men do on dark nights with unbroken horses in very broken country; but I didn't try to tell the busman about them.

> What do they understand?
> Beefy face and grubby 'and.

He went on placidly, 'Ah, London for me; all the luxuries of the world come to London; the best of everythink's good enough for us; and it's a healthy place too. Look at me. I'm past 50 and I'm 16 hours a day on this bus.'

I thought he must have a lot of time to enjoy luxuries.

The Public and the Politicians

Public affairs here are conducted on quite a different basis from ours; here, a political career, like the army, is a matter for the 'classes'—wealthy or respectable—and the public don't bother themselves much about the

politicians, and the latter certainly don't bother them-
selves at all about the public. To give an example. The
Buller affair is just now making as much commotion as
anything can make in this vast wilderness. The papers
and records dealing with Buller are all known to be at
the War Office, and the whole question could be settled
in five minutes. The public ask—at least, they don't ask
really because they are too apathetic, but we would ex-
pect them to ask—(1) Did Buller make blunders in Af-
rica sufficient to justify his recall? (2) If so, why was he
appointed to command the First Army Corps? (3) Being
so appointed, why was he dismissed?

I was talking this over with an English gentleman
interested in political matters and having considerable
knowledge of affairs. He said, 'Of course we know, and
the newspapers know, all the facts about Buller, and the
papers can be seen by us, but not officially. The Ministry
have thought it better not to publish them. If they do
publish them—' and he left it to be inferred that things
would be very bad for Buller. I said, 'Why don't the public
insist on their publishing them?' I saw a hundred
thousand people in Hyde Park—certainly most of them
had only gone there for what is to them a day's sport in
the country—to go into Hyde Park and boohoo at the
mention of Lord Roberts—but still they were there, and
the press are trying to raise a clamour about Buller, and
the music hall singers are getting great applause for
'extra verses' about Buller and yet no one knows in the
least how the affair really stands.

He said, with an air of settling the matter, 'But I told
you the Ministry don't think it worthwhile to publish the
papers.'

Public Indifference

'Well,' I said, 'in Australia, if anything as important as
this occurred, there would be a dozen members of Parlia-
ment who would go and demand the papers, and would

tell their constituents what was the truth. There would
be a member on every step of the War Office stairs waiting
till it opened in the morning and a howling crowd of
their constituents outside.'

After hearing him, and seeing a few things for myself,
I began to realise how it was that the favouritism and
contemptuous disregard for public interest that we
constantly saw in Africa could go unremarked and un-
checked. It appears to be nobody's business to interpose.
England and Australia are at the two extremes in political
matters. Here a general may half wreck an Empire and
no one does anything; with us if a sergeant of Volunteers
is disrated for drunkenness there is a Labour member to
demand a special committee of the House to inquire into
it. Those are the two systems, and each has its drawbacks.
You pay your money and don't have any choice.

I went to the War Office, the centre of public indif-
ference in London just now (you can't say public interest,
because there is no public interest that one can see); one
would expect to find it besieged by a crowd of people,
considering that the war is in full swing; one would expect
to find inventors with new explosives; colonels with new
schemes to end the war; politicians with blunt axes that
wanted grinding. Instead of that a peaceful, tranquil calm
rested over the place. I appeared to be the only visitor
they had that day. Truly it is an amazing country.

Where Australians Abound

If one knows where to go and look for them London holds
a fair number of Australians, and curiously enough they
are nearly all engaged in music, literature, or art of some
sort. Are we an artistic nation? One would be forced to
that conclusion by visiting the artistic circles here. In
other circles it is the greatest rarity to meet an Aus-
tralian; in these circles they abound, and all appear to do
fairly well. Our artists come over and grimly set to work
at any work they can get at any rate of pay they can

command—a proceeding that does not commend itself to the 'established' artists, who are getting their ten or twenty pounds a page for inferior work—work that sells because of the name and not because of its merit. By-and-by the Australian works up, till he, too, gets his ten or twenty pounds a page. The same with the singers. The girls come over here and go into humble little lodgings and work hard—oh, so hard—on the few pounds of capital that their friends have got together for them. They take all sorts of small concert engagements and before long they always seem to drop into some steady work, and one characteristic thing is that they always help each other. Melba, Ada Crossley, Florence Schmidt, and the others who have succeeded are always ready to give a hand to their countrywomen who have only started to make their way; and the same is the case with the artists. In fact, all our national representatives who are doing well themselves are not disposed to forget others. But none of them like the life here, the terrifically hard work, the impossibility of getting any exercise, fresh air, or change.

Amy Castle's debut was a great Australian function, but her friends rather made a mistake in 'packing' the hall and making it apparent that the 'success' and 'enthusiasm' were all arranged beforehand. The general public rather resented it. The girl's singing is wonderful and at another concert, when she sang just before a leading concert soprano well known in London, the contrast in the two performances was all in Amy Castles' favour. The other girl had to strive visibly for her high notes but Amy Castles just simply opened her mouth and the notes came—a regular flood of melody, with the impression of great reserve power behind it, which is such a charm in a singer.

Everyone Has a Chance

That is one of the greatest fascinations of London life— the fact that everyone has a chance, for all are treated alike with indifference, and there is no royal road to a success. Kubelik the violinist came here an unknown foreigner and played at a cheap concert as a start. Down in Australia we are apt to read inflated cablegrams, and get an undue idea of our own importance; the debut of an Australian singer is not an important event. The singers of all nations 'debut' here at the rate of about four a day; the night before Amy Castles there appeared a new Russian singer, and the night after an Austrian Princess made her first (and, it is whispered, probably her last) appearance on a concert platform. They fall into London like hail into a pond, and one debutante more or less makes just about as much difference as one hail-stone more or less. Our Australian view of it is rather like that of an old back-block friend of mine, a butcher up Walgett way, who sent his son down to Sydney at the time of the Jubilee celebration. When the hopeful came back—after seeing the crowds and the festivities, mostly from the top of a bus—the old man said, with great complacency, 'Well, Bill, what did they think of yer in Sydney? I suppose they were all talkin' about yer?' And Bill was silent.

I have never seen more than a few lines of Australian news in any paper, and very rarely does any at all appear. Australia is the least known place in the world here; the London press are beginning to take some interest in it now, mainly because of the visit of the Prince and Princess of Wales.

We get good fun out of meeting men from other parts of the world sometimes; each gets telling the other about the place he comes from, and before long each tries to outdo the other in stories. The latest is that an Australian and an Indian met at a club and the talk was on grass. 'Grass? my dear fellow,' said the Indian, 'I've positively seen grass so high and thick that the elephants couldn't force their way through it. Positively couldn't get along, I assure you!' The Australian drew at his pipe for one second, and then said in a hushed voice, 'Would you mind changing the subject? Ever since I was out in the Territory (pause)—and a blade of grass fell on a friend of mine and killed him—I hate talking about grass.'

Sydney Morning Herald, 11 January 1902

In Push Society

... 'Where to, sir?' asked the cabman.

'Nearest dancing saloon,' said Gordon, briefly.

'Nearest darncin' saloon,' said the cabman. 'There ain't no parties to-night, sir; it's too 'ot.'

'We're not expecting to drop into a ballroom without being asked, thank you,' said Gordon. 'We want to go to one of those saloons where you pay a shilling to go in. Some place where the larrikins go.'

'Ho! is that it, sir?' said the cabman, with a grin. 'Well, I'll take you to a noo place, most selectest place I know. Git up, 'orse.' And off they rattled through the quiet streets, turning corners and crossing tramlines every fifty yards, apparently, and bumping against each other in the most fraternal manner.

Soon the cab pulled up in a narrow, ill-lit street, at the open door of a dingy house. Instructing the cabman to wait, they hustled upstairs, to be confronted at the top by a man who took a shilling from each, and then was not sure whether he would admit them. He didn't seem to like their form exactly, and muttered something to a by-stander as they went in. They saw a long, low room, brilliantly lighted by flaring gas jets. Down one side, on wooden forms, was seated a row of flashily dressed girls— larrikinesses on their native heath, barmaids from cheap, disreputable hotels, shop girls, factory girls—all sharp-faced and pert, young in years, but old in knowledge of evil. The demon of mischief peeped out of their quick-moving restless eyes. They had elaborate fringes, and their short dresses exhibited well-turned ankles and legs.

A large notice on the wall stated that 'Gentlemen must not dance with nails in their boots. Gentlemen must not dance together.'

'That blocks us,' said Gordon, pointing to the notice. 'Can't dance together, no matter how much we want to. Look at these fellows here.'

Opposite the women sat or lounged a score or two of youths—wiry, hard-faced little fellows, for the most part, with scarcely a sizeable man amongst them. They were all clothed in 'push' evening dress—black bell-bottomed pants, no waistcoat, very short black paget coat, white shirt with no collar, and a gaudy neckerchief round the bare throat. Their boots were marvels, very high in the heel and picked out with all sorts of colours down the sides. They looked 'varminty' enough for anything; but the shifty eyes, low foreheads, and evil faces gave our two heroes a sense of disgust. The Englishman thought that all the stories he had heard of the Australian larrikin must be exaggerated, and that any man who was at all athletic could easily hold his own among such a poor-looking lot. The whole spectacle was disappointing. The most elaborately decorous order prevailed; no excitement or rough play was noticeable, and their expedition seemed likely to be a failure.

The bushman stared down the room with far-seeing eyes, apparently looking at nothing, and contemplated the whole show with bored indifference.

'Nothing very dazzling about this,' he said. 'I'm afraid we can't show you anything very exciting here. Better go back to the club, eh?'

Just then the band (piano and violin) struck up a slow, laboured waltz, 'Bid me goodbye and go,' and each black-coated male, with languid self-possession, strolled across the room, seized a lady by the arm, jerked her to her

feet without saying a syllable, and commenced to dance
in slow, convulsive movements, making a great many
revolutions for very little progress. Two or three girls
were left sitting, as their partners were talking in a little
knot at the far end of the room; one among them was
conspicuously pretty, and she began to ogle Carew in a
very pronounced way.

'There's one hasn't got a partner,' said Gordon. 'Good-
looking Tottie, too. Go and ask her to dance. See what
she says.'

The Englishman hesitated for a second. 'I don't like
asking a perfect stranger to dance,' he said.

'Go on,' said Gordon, 'it's all right. She'll like it.'

Carew drew down his cuffs, squared his shoulders,
assumed his most absolutely stolid drawing-room man-
ner, and walked across the room, a gleaming vision of
splendour in his immaculate evening dress.

'May I—er—have the pleasure of this dance?' he said,
with elaborate politeness.

The girl giggled a little, but said nothing, then rose
and took his arm.

As she did so, a youth among the talkers at the other
end of the room looked round, and stared for a second.
Then he moistened his fingers with his tongue, smoothed
the hair on his temples, and with elbows held out from
his sides, shoulders hunched up, and under-jaw stuck
well out, bore down on Carew and the girl, who were get-
ting under way when he came up. Taking not the slight-
est notice of Carew, he touched the girl on the shoulder
with a sharp peremptory tap, and brought their dance to
a stop.

''Ere,' he said, in commanding tones. ''Oo are you
darncin' with?'

'I'm darncin' with 'im,' answered the girl, pertly, indi-
cating the Englishman with a jerk of her head.

'Ho, you're darncin' with 'im, are you? 'E brought you
'ere, p'r'aps?'

'No, he didn't,' she said.

'No,' he said. ''You know well enough 'e didn't.'

While this conversation was going on, the Englishman maintained an attitude of dignified reserve, leaving it to the lady to decide who was to be the favoured man. At last he felt it was hardly right for an Oxford man, and a triple blue at that, to be discussed in this contemptuous way by a larrikin and his 'donah', so he broke into the discussion, perhaps a little abruptly, but using his most polished style.

'I—ah—asked this lady to dance, and if she—er—will do me the honour,' he said, 'I—'

'Oh! you arst 'er to darnce? And what right 'ad you to arst 'er to darnce, you lop-eared rabbit?' interrupted the larrikin, raising his voice as he warmed to his subject. 'I brought 'er 'ere. I paid the shillin'. Now then, you take your 'ook,' he went on, pointing sternly to the door, and talking as he would to a disobedient dog. 'Go on, now. Take your 'ook.'

The Englishman said nothing, but his jaw set ominously. The girl giggled, delighted at being the centre of so much observation. The band stopped playing, and the dancers crowded round. Word was passed down that it was a 'toff darncin' with Nugget's donah', and from various parts of the room black-coated duplicates of Nugget hurried swiftly to the scene.

The doorkeeper turned to Gordon. 'You'd best get your mate out o' this,' he said. 'These are the Rocks Push, and they'll deal with him all right.'

'Deal with him, will they?' said Gordon, looking at the gesticulating Nugget. 'They'll bite off more than they can chew if they interfere with him. This is just his form, a row like this. He's a bit of a champion in a rough-and-tumble, I believe.'

'Is he?' said the doorkeeper, sardonically. 'Well, look 'ere, now, you take it from me, if there's a row Nugget will spread him out as flat as a newspaper. They've all been in the ring in their time, these coves. There's Nugget and Ginger, and Brummy—all red 'ot. You get him away!'

Meanwhile the Englishman's ire was gradually rising. He was past the stage of considering whether it was worth while to have a fight over a factory girl in a shilling dancing saloon, and the desire for battle blazed up in his eyes. He turned and confronted Nugget.

'You go about your business,' he said, dropping all the laboured politeness out of his tones. 'If she likes to dance —'

He got no further. A shrill whistle rang through the room; a voice shouted, 'Don't 'it 'im; 'ook 'im!' His arms were seized from behind and pinioned to his sides. The lights were turned out. Somebody in front hit him a terrific crack in the eye at the same moment that someone else administered a violent kick from the rear. He was propelled by an invisible force to the head of the stairs, and then—whizz! down he went in one prodigious leap, clear from the top to the first landing.

Here, in pitch-darkness, he grappled one of his assailants. For a few seconds they swayed and struggled, and then rolled down the rest of the stairs, over and over each other, grappling and clawing, each trying to tear the other's shirt off. When they rolled into the street, Carew discovered that he had hold of Charlie Gordon.

They sat up and looked at each other. Then they made a simultaneous rush for the stairs, but the street door was slammed in their faces. They kicked it violently, but without result, except that a mob of faces looked out of the first-floor window and hooted, and a bucket of water was emptied over them. A crowd collected as if by magic, and the spectacle of two gentlemen in evening dress trying to kick in the door of a shilling dancing saloon afforded it unmitigated delight.

''Ere's two toffs got done in all right,' said one.

'What O! Won't she darnce with you?' said another; and somebody from the back threw banana peel at them.

Charlie recovered his wits first. The Englishman was fairly berserk with rage, and glared round on the by-standers as if he contemplated a rush among them. The cabman put an end to the performance. He was tranquil and unemotional, and he soothed them down and coaxed them into the cab. The band in the room above resumed the dreamy waltz music of 'Bid me goodbye and go!' and they went.

Carew subsided into the corner, breathing hard and feeling his eye. Charlie leant forward and peered out into the darkness. They were nearly at the club before they spoke. Then he said, 'Well, I'm blessed! We made a nice mess of that, didn't we?'

'I'd like to have got one fair crack at some of 'em,' said the Englishman, with heartfelt earnestness. 'Couldn't we go back now?'

'No, what's the good? We'd never get in. Let the thing alone. We needn't say anything about it. If once it gets known that we were chucked out, we'll never hear the last of it. Are you marked at all?'

'Got an awful swipe in the eye,' replied the other briefly.

'I've got a cut lip, and my head nearly screwed off. You did that. I'll know the place again. Some day we'll get a few of the right sort to come with us, and we'll just go there quietly, as if we didn't mean anything, and then, all of a sudden, we'll turn in and break the whole place up! Come and have a drink now.'

They had a silent drink in the deserted club. The mind of each was filled with a sickening sense of defeat, and without much conversation they retired to bed. They thanked heaven that the Bo'sun, Pinnock, and even Gillespie had disappeared.

Chapter 3, *An Outback Marriage*, 1906

THE COOK-HOUSE

Our unit is a Base unit, and does not have to bustle and shift about; our cook-house, therefore, is more a permanent structure than is usual with Army cook-houses. It consists of a brick oven, frequently out of action, half a dozen Sawyer—or should it be Sayer—stoves, a brick-floored, mat-sided, reed-roofed shed, a meat-house, and a mat shed, used indifferently by the cook-house gang as a debating hall, a gymnasium, and a shelter from the heat. Here, when the day's work is over, the wits of the squadron assemble and discuss various topics in the cool of the evening. Anybody can have, at any hour of the day or night, a drink of tea, an argument, a punch on the nose, or a duel of wits, by applying at our cook-house. Not that there is much, or, indeed, any fighting ever done there, though, to hear the talk, one would expect to see about six fights a day. The fights never come off, though they are there if you want them; and all the talk of fight is good-natured banter, intended to pass the time pleasantly and to draw out whatever mother-wit there may be in the troops.

Our work as a unit consists in the supply of helmets and steel burnishers for bits and stirrup irons to the Australian Forces. So we are not a very popular unit; but such as our work is, we do it to the best of our ability; and we are enabled to employ a number of middle-aged men, too old for the fighting line. Thus our cook is well over forty-five and has run to flesh somewhat; he is an old soldier and knows how to carry himself; and only that his chest has slipped down a bit, he still has a fine military figure. During his years of military service he has learnt how to handle men. So he affects a ferocity of demeanour and language that serves its purpose by keeping the younger men in order; while he is quite ready, nay, even eager, to enter into an argument with the seasoned old soldiers, who tell him to 'cut out the bluff and talk sense'. In private life he is a quiet and successful tradesman, whose life is devoid of incident; but here he has to cope every day with the problem of feeding two hundred hungry Australians, some of whom have known the best, and others the worst, cooking in the world. As he says himself, 'It's not the blokes that lived at the Hotel Australia that grumble; it's the men that's been in the Northern Territory, livin' on waterlily roots and goannas, cooked by black gins!' But he does not lose any sleep over the grumblers—not like the French king's cook who hanged himself because the fish was not done enough. Our cook would persuade any grumblers that they did not know the right way to cook fish!

His staff consists of three—an offsider, who is supposed to understudy the cook, and two helpers, who cut wood, peel vegetables, wash pots, carry firewood, and do the hundred and one other jobs of a cook-house in a Base camp. As birds of a feather flock together, so the cook has got round him the philosophers and sages of the unit. His offsider is a bushman of the old school, a tall, lean and very old giant, who has carried a swag to many a station and swung a pick in many a mine, always on the new rushes and to the far out stations. He is silent, shrewd, and good-natured to a fault. He it was who cut out the pictures from the Australian weeklies—oddly varied here and there by cuttings from *La Vie Parisienne* —and pasted them on the cook-house walls. When you come to think of it, no true outback Australian cook could possibly inhabit a cook-house for long without pasting some pictures round it. His taste in illustrations follows the old groove, and the present-day Australian racehorses and high-jumpers look out in effigy on the grey Egyptian desert. His part in the daily cook-house comedy is that of the oracle of Delphos. If anybody comes up looking for a fight, they are told they must fight Donnelly; if any very knotty point arises in argument, it is always referred to Donnelly; and many a grumbler has had to go away, snorting under the assurance that his grievance will be reported to Donnelly first thing in the morning. Donnelly is supposed to have fought all the leading pugilists, beaten all the leading runners, to have dug up the biggest nuggets, and to have had more adventures of an amorous nature than Don Juan. With true Australian fatalism, he meekly accepts this outlandish role, and always plays up to the cook in business and dialogue without any previous rehearsal. 'It keeps the boys amused,' he says.

The other two members of the cook-house are cast for thinking parts (as the actors have it), and say nothing, except that they come in occasionally, like the chorus of a Greek play, with observations that lend point and confirmation to their chief's arguments—one of them, it should be mentioned, is a pocket Hercules, as fearless as a bulldog; and everyone knows that, if they really went looking for trouble in the cook-house, they could easily find it; consequently, nobody ever looks for it, and the most bloodthirsty threats are taken as they are meant to be, in a purely figurative and diplomatic sense.

Let us suppose, now, it is after tea in camp. The boiling Egyptian sun has slid down into his couch of fleecy clouds and the cool desert breeze brings life and cheerfulness on its wings. The cook-house gang, all smoking, sit on the form outside their shed, prepared to take on anybody. A fair sprinkling of men are lounging about, smoking after tea, and there is a constant coming and going of men from the tents. A dixie of water is simmering on the fire, and this has to be kept to make the tea for a detachment of men, who have been away delivering helmets and steel burnishers to brother Australians further up the line. There is a concert on at an adjoining camp, where many 'sisters' will be present; so every man who has leave for the concert wants to get some of that hot water to shave with. And first comes up one, 'Bluey', a character, mug in hand, and sidles towards the dixie, with one eye on the cook.

'Now then, "Bluey",' says the cook, 'cut it out! You can't have none of that water. I want it for the boys that are coming in late.'

'Bluey' is a large, red-headed, good natured youth, full of *joie de vivre*, and, occasionally, other liquids; he is no debater, but is always ready to join in any sort of rough-house gambols that will serve to help the afternoon performance along. He puts his mug on the ground, and adopting an exaggerated version of the Hughie Mehegan smother, he advances on the cook-house.

'Now then,' says he, 'I've fought and beat every man in this cook-house, except one.'

'Which one is that?'

'Donnelly! Come on, Donnelly, you've lived too long! Come out here and stack your apparel, till I kill you.'

The words 'till I kill you' are apparently Donnelly's cue, as he at once takes the stage and grapples with the intruder. They wrestle and bump about among the stoves and firewood. The spectators cheer impartially. 'Stay with him, Donnelly!' 'Good on you, "Bluey"!' 'Uppercut him, "Bluey"!' 'Come off the stove!' From distant tents come hoarse cries of encouragement: 'Choke him!' 'Put the boot in, Donnelly!' And so on. After a while, the Cook, seeing that the 'turn' has lasted long enough, signals to his next in rank. 'Jack,' he says, 'go over there and throw that man "Bluey" out. Donnelly might kill him.'

Jack makes a short rush, puts his arms around the struggling pair, and rushes them out into the open. Here 'Bluey' is sorted out from his antagonist, his mug is thrown after him, and he disappears from the stage, not without applause.

Next comes a tall, angular, morose-looking soldier, very dirty. He is known as 'The Nark', being a man of trouble-making disposition; on more than one occasion he has put in a complaint to the orderly officer about the cookery. He has a great flow of invective, and spectators rouse themselves in anticipation as he bears down on the cook-house. The cook, on the principle that attack is the best defence, gets in the first shot.

'Now, "Nark", what do you want? It's no good your comin' after water. You'd only say that it wasn't boiled the way you like it.'

The audience laugh but 'The Nark' regards the cook coldly, and says nothing. Following up his initial success, the cook is emboldened to further flights.

'Ho,' he says, '"The Nark's" a good soldier. When you roust on him, and he knows he's in the wrong, he don't answer back; just stands there and takes it.'

'The Nark' shows his teeth in a dry grin. 'Was you roustin' on me?' he inquires, in great surprise.

'Corse I was roustin' on you. Who else would I be roustin' on?'

'I thought most likely you were talkin' to some of those pot-washin' staff coves of yours. They want roustin' on. If the whole lot of you went cookin' in a shearin' shed, you'd be lynched.'

'You hear that, Donnelly?' says the cook, in horror. 'He says you wouldn't cook for shearers! You that was voted in as cook seven years runnin' in the biggest shed in Queensland, with two hundred shearers! Wasn't you, Donnelly?'

'I suppose I was,' says Donnelly. But 'The Nark', like a good General, throws all his forces on the weakest point of defence.

'Donnelly,' he says 'put in most of his life helping to put new roofs on public houses!' And with this parting blow, which is generally conceded to be somewhat of a bit below the belt, he slouches off the dishonours of War.

Next comes a little London cockney, who has joined up with us in Australia. He has the Londoner's readiness of tongue.

'Cook,' he says, as he swaggers up, 'why don't you call those men of yours to attention when I come past? I'll 'ave that stripe off you, if you ain't careful!'

'I'll put Donnelly on to you,' says the cook, for want of any better retort.

'I'll job Donnelly on the bread-basket. Why ain't he boilin' up some water for me, instead of loafin' there!'

'Why don't you go out and pinch some firewood and I'll give you plenty 'ot water?'

'Garn! If there was enough of you here to put up a decent fight with me, I'd go in and knock the lot of you.'

Thud! Thud! Thud! Three bad potatoes, skilfully thrown by the cook-house gang, land on him like machine gun fire, and he ducks and bolts off, to the accompaniment of Homeric laughter from the troops.

'There you are,' says the cook. 'I was keeping them potatoes to show the orderly officer, and you go and waste them on that!'

But now there is a tramp of feet in the gloom, and the detachment marches in, hungry, tired and bad-tempered, as men are after a long day in the Egyptian sun. While they are having a wash, the cook bustles about dealing out the stew, and making tea. Two mess orderlies come up to draw the stew, and the cook ladles out the steaming mixture. The first man gets his allowance and departs and the cook, glancing casually into the stew-pot, says, 'How many have you got, Mick?'

Mick is a harassed youth who takes everything seriously.

'Nine, and all gormandisers,' he says.

'Do they like ungyuns?'

'Yes, I suppose so.'

'Well, here you are then. There's a beautiful lot of ungyuns in this.' And the cook ladles out a mixture in which the 'ungyuns' advertise themselves with no un-certain voice. The mess orderly has learnt to fear Greeks bringing gifts, so he inspects the dish narrowly.

'Why,' he says, 'it's all onions. There's hardly any meat.'

'Go on! There's plenty meat. And you said you wanted plenty ungyuns.'

And the mess orderly retreats with his steaming dish, merely pausing to throw over his shoulder the remark, addressed apparently to the universe in general, 'Cooks always is the lowest dorgs in the Army!'

But the cook takes no notice. The day's work is over, and turning to Donnelly, he asks him whether he thinks he could keep one down; and Donnelly feeling equal to the task, they go off to the canteen together.

From 'Army Sketches' in the
Kia-Ora Coo-ee, 15 October 1918

Concerning a Dog Fight

Dog fighting as a sport is not much in vogue nowadays. To begin with, it is illegal. Not that *that* matters much, for Sunday drinking is also illegal, yet flourishes exceedingly. But dog fighting is one of the cruel sports which the united sense of the community has decided to put down with all the force of public opinion. Nevertheless, a certain amount of dog fighting is still carried on around Sydney and very neatly and scientifically carried on, too— principally by gentlemen who follow the occupation of slaughterers, and who live out Botany way and do not care for public opinion.

The grey dawn was just breaking over Botany when we got to the meeting place. It was Sunday morning, and all the respectable, non-dog fighting population of that stinking suburb were sleeping the heavy, Sunday morning sleep. Away to the east the stars were paling at the first faint flush of the coming dawn, and over the sandhills

came the boom of the breakers. An intense stillness was
over everything, and the white-walled cottages of Botany
were shrouded in a faint mist. Some few people, how-
ever, were astir. In the dim light, hurried pedestrians
might be seen plodding their way over the heavy road
towards the sandhills. Now and then a van, laden with
about 10 or 11 of 'the talent', and drawn by a horse that
cost 15s. at auction, rolled softly along in the same di-
rection. These were dog fighters who had got 'the office',
and knew exactly where the chewing match was to take
place.

The 'meet' was on a main road, about half a mile from
town, and here some 200 people had assembled, and hung
up their horses and vehicles to the fence without the
slightest concealment. They said the police would not
interfere with them, and in truth, they did not seem a
nice crowd to interfere with. One dog was on the ground
when we arrived. He had come out in a hansom cab with
his trainer, and was a white bull terrier, weighing about
40 pounds, 'trained to the hour', with the muscles standing
out all over him. He waited in the cab, and licked his
trainer's face at intervals, to reassure that individual of
his protection and support. The rest of the time he
glowered out of the cab and eyed the public scornfully.
He knew as well as any human being that there was
sport afoot, and he looked about eagerly and wickedly to
see what he could get his teeth into. Then a messenger
came running up to the cab and demanded to know, with
a variety of expletives, whether they meant to sit in the
cab till the police came; also, he said that the other dog
had arrived and all was ready. The trainer and dog got
out of the cab, and we followed through a fence and over
a rise, and there, about 200 yards from the main road,
was a neatly pitched enclosure like a prize ring—i.e. a
30-foot square enclosure formed with stakes and ropes.
About a hundred people were at the ringside, and in the

far corner, in the arms of his trainer, was the other dog—
a brindle.

It was wonderful to see the two dogs when they caught
sight of each other. The white dog came up to the ring
straining at his leash, nearly dragging his trainer off his
feet in his efforts to get at the enemy. At intervals he
emitted a hoarse roar of challenge and defiance. The
brindled dog never uttered a sound. He fixed his eyes on
his adversary with a look of intense hunger, of absolute
yearning for combat. He never for an instant shifted his
unwinking gaze. He seemed like an animal who saw the
hopes of years about to be realised. With painful earnest-
ness he watched every detail of the other dog's toilet; and
while the white dog was making fierce efforts to get at
him, he stood Napoleonic, grand in his courage, waiting
for the fray.

All details were carefully attended to, and all rules
strictly observed. Most people think a dog fight is a
go-as-you-please outbreak of lawlessness, but there are
rules and regulations—simple, but effective. Possibly one
could even buy a book containing the rules of dog fight-
ing. There were two umpires, a referee, a timekeeper,
and two seconds for each dog. The stakes were said to be
ten pounds a side. After some talk, the dogs were carried
to the centre of the ring by their seconds and put on the
ground. Like a flash of lightning they dashed at each
other, and the fight began. Nearly everyone has seen
dogs fight—'it is their nature to', as Dr. Watts puts it.
But an ordinary worry between (say) a retriever and a
collie, terminating as soon as one or other gets his ear
bitten, gives a very faint idea of a real dog fight. These
bull terriers are the gladiators of the canine race. Bred
and trained to fight, carefully exercised and dieted for
weeks beforehand, they come to the fray exulting in their
strength and each determined to win. Each is trained to
fight for certain holds, a grip of the ear or the back of

the neck being of very slight importance. The foot is a favourite hold; the throat is, of course, fashionable—if they can get it. These dogs sparred and wrestled and gripped and threw each other, fighting grimly, and disdaining to utter a sound under the most severe punishment. Their seconds dodged round them unceasingly, giving them encouragement and advice. 'That's the style, Boxer—fight for his foot.' 'Draw your foot back, old man', and so on. Now and again one dog got a grip of the other's foot and chewed savagely, and the spectators danced with excitement. The moment the dogs released hold of each other they were snatched up by their seconds and carried to their corners, and a minute's time was allowed, in which their mouths were washed out and a cloth rubbed over their bodies.

Then came the ceremony of 'coming to scratch'. After the first round, on time being called, the brindled dog was let loose in his own corner of the ring, and he was required by the rules to go across the ring (some 30 ft.) of his own free will and attack the other dog. If he failed to do this he would lose the fight. The white dog, meanwhile, was held in his corner waiting the attack. After the next round it was the white dog's turn to make the attack, and so on alternately. It, therefore, became evident that the animals need not fight a moment longer than they chose, as either dog could abandon the fight by failing to go across the ring and attack his enemy. While their condition lasted they used to dash across the ring at full run, but after a while, when the punishment got severe and their 'fitness' began to fail, it became a very exciting question whether or not a dog would 'come to scratch'. The brindled dog's condition was not so good as the other's, and he used to be on his stomach between the rounds to rest himself, and it several times looked as if he would not cross the ring when his turn came. But as soon as time was called he would start to his feet and come limping slowly across glaring steadily at the other dog; then as he got nearer, he would quicken his pace and at last make a savage rush, and in a moment they would be locked in combat. So they battled on for 56 minutes till the white dog (who was apparently having all the best of it), on being called on to cross the ring, only went halfway across and stood there growling savagely till a minute had elapsed, and so he lost the fight.

No doubt it was a brutal exhibition. But it was not cruel to the animals in the same sense that pigeon shooting or hare hunting is cruel. The dogs are born fighters, anxious and eager to fight, desiring nothing better. Whatever limited intelligence they have is all directed to this one consuming passion. They could stop when they liked, but anyone looking on could see that they gloried in the combat. Fighting is like breath to them—they must have it. Nature has implanted in all animals a fighting instinct for the weeding out of the physically unfit, and these dogs have an extra share of that fighting instinct. Of course, now that the world is going to be so good, and we are all to be teetotal and only fight in debating societies, and the women are to wear the breeches, these nasty, savage animals are out of date, and we will not be allowed to have anything more quarrelsome than a poodle about the house—though even poodles will fight like demons when they feel like it. And the gamecock and the steeplechase-horse and all animals with sporting or fighting instincts must be done away with. Guinea pigs will, perhaps, be safe to keep, though even *they* have a go-in at one another occasionally. And the man of the future, the New Man, whose fighting instincts are not quite bred out of him, will, perhaps, be found at a grey dawn of a Sunday morning with a crowd of other unregenerates in some backyard frantically cheering on two determined buck guinea pigs to mortal combat.

THE WAYS OF THE WILD

The Dog-Poisoner: A Bush Sketch

In the Australian bush a dingo is always a 'dorg'. Anywhere west of the Zoo they never talk of dingoes but when a man's run is infested by dingoes they say he has 'dorgs' in on him. A cattle dog is a heeler, and a sheep dog is a collie; but a dingo is always a 'dorg'.

To have dorgs in on you is worse than drought, low prices and an overdraft all combined. The amount of damage that a dingo can do not only by killing but by rushing and demoralising the sheep, is almost incredible. When dingoes get into a paddock the sheep break up into small scattered mobs, rush blindly like hares at the slightest sound and seem to lose even the small amount of sense that they usually possess. Once dogs are in on sheep everything else must be dropped till they are got rid of; and for this purpose the hour produces the man. There is always in every district at least one man who is skilled in the ways of 'dorgs'. Generally he is a useless person in other respects but when the dingoes come about he is the Napoleon of the occasion.

See him now, called into consultation with the boss when word is brought in that sheep have been killed in a paddock. Long and sinewy, slow in speech and deliberate in action, the dog-poisoner strolls up to the homestead to advise on the plan of campaign.

The boss has no love for the dog-poisoner, for the latter is usually a wild man, a hunter by instinct, preferring to trap rabbits, shoot foxes or do a bit of bark-stripping for a living, rather than settle down to regular toil. Also he owns no sheep but never goes short of mutton; but he is the only refuge in time of trouble, and the boss calls this strange ally into council hoping for the best.

'There's a dog in on the nine-mile paddocks, Donnelly, two or three of them by the look of things. What do you think we had better do?'

Donnelly has already got word by bush wireless that a dog has shown up, and he has already laid out a plan of campaign; but the great unhurried methods of the bush must be followed and he discusses the matter as if it were news to him.

'A dorg in, eh? Anyone seen him?'

'No, but there's three or four sheep dead, bitten in the flank and left. Just killed for sport or spite. No doubt it's a dingo; what had we better do?'

Now there are three or four ways of tackling a dingo, either by poison, shooting, trapping or driving; and not any way is very satisfactory, for the dingo is far ahead of the English fox in cunning. A fox is an easy proposition to get rid of, compared to a dingo, for a fox will take any poison that is stuck in the head of a bird and in regard to traps he is not much harder to deceive than a rabbit, but a dingo will take no bait on which there is the slightest human smell; he can smell a trap even though it be buried underground; and when a drive is on foot the breeze seems to carry the news to him, and he will be out of the district before the drivers have properly got started. There is no animal more intelligent than the dingo, and the dog-poisoner has a foeman worthy of his steel.

The poisoner, having made up his mind to try baits and traps, says languidly:

'How about a drive? If you put the guns up along the top of the big hill he'd be sure to make up that way—'

'Drive! How the deuce can we get men for a drive? There isn't a chance, besides he'll have half the sheep on the place killed while you are fixing it up.'

'Well, I don't know if I can spare the time to go out there myself. I've got a contract to strip a couple of hundred sheets of bark . . .'

'Oh, never mind the bark. I'll give you a fiver if you get him; and that will pay you better than bark. When can you go out? I've no doubt the next run will chip in a pound or two as well.'

The dog-poisoner thinks it over.

'Well, if you can let me have an old horse to pack me traps and gear out, and a bit of tucker, and if you'll send Billy down to draw a bit of wood for the old woman while I'm away, and me own little mare is lame and I don't know what to do with her. I've got nowhere to put her without I could put her in your lower paddock—'

Quicker than an American Peace Conference terms are concluded. When dorgs are in, the poisoner can dictate his own terms.

Out in the great silent ranges under the shelter of a cliff, the poisoner puts up his fly of a tent, rakes together a few armfuls of candle-bark for his bed, and prepares his traps and baits. A dog trap is a formidable affair that will very nearly hold a horse, should it get its foot fast in those cruel jaws. Riding far away from his camp, he selects a spot on a 'pad' or sheep track, for a dingo will always run along a pad rather than cut across country. Here the trap is carefully set and covered with earth and a few leaves are burnt over it to drive away any human scent. Then a few drops of dingo lure—every poisoner has some sort of lure that he believes in—are scattered about and the trap is ready. Here and there in likely places, as he makes his way back to his camp, the poisoner lays baits made of the contents of a sardine tin, mixed with a little fat and seasoned with strychnine. Mr. Kipling says there are nine and fifty ways of constructing tribal lays and there are as many ways of getting baits for dingoes. A favourite way is to stick the mixture into the crevices of a log with a pocket knife in an accidental sort of way. A dog will often lick up one of these accidental baits, while he would pass a bait displayed in the open.

Next day, and perhaps for many days after, the poisoner goes the rounds of his traps and his baits, renewing the latter and trying all sorts of dodges to get the quarry to put his foot in a trap. Sometimes a sheep's head is buried underground and the trap set on top of it. The smell of the buried meat attracts the dog and he scratches away the soil to see what is underneath. That is the end of him.

While the hunt is on the poisoner sleeps out in the ranges, often in snow and frost, seeing nobody, reading nothing and passing his time in smoking and meditation. Then comes the day when patience is rewarded and a dog stiff in death is picked up near the site of one of the baits or a snapping, springing victim is despatched in a trap by a blow of a stirrup iron.

Then the poisoner returns to civilisation and casts down the skin with the remark, 'There's your dorg.'

As for the five or six pounds reward—well, a fiver means about a decent week's drinking. The poisoner is a primitive man with a primitive man's ways of enjoying himself.

Sydney Sportsman, 27 February 1922

The Banjo v. Henry Lawson

So you're back from up the country, Mister Lawson...

Henry Lawson

It is surprising that Paterson's account of how the battle of the ballads between himself and Henry Lawson in 1892 came about has so often been brushed aside. For some critics the conflict has helped towards a tidy categorisation of the two men; in the left corner, the tribune of the people, Henry Lawson, and in the right corner the languid spokesman for the squatters, A.B. Paterson. Scraps of verse have been extracted to underpin the seriousness of this thesis.

However, when the full texts are read, especially Lawson's, the jokey nature of the duel is evident, which is why his verses are reproduced in this selection along with Paterson's. Lawson cheerfully and floridly overwrites to the point of parody: 'Where in clouds of dust enveloped, roasted bullock-drivers creep.' He pads out the lines outrageously, as does The Banjo, in pursuit of extra shillings. One wonders why Archibald let them get away with it, but then he probably saw the joke, as did a couple of lesser poets who joined in.

While Lawson flails the squatter, he is also unkind to the labour 'agitator'. There are enough personal barbs, to be sure. (Modest critics have avoided comment on Lawson's broad suggestion that Paterson was visiting the seamstresses in their attics for immoral purposes.) The Banjo's irony about Lawson's professions of liking for lemon-squash are to the point. But in the end Lawson, in a last postscript, turns in a few lines as sentimental concerning the bush and riding as anything The Banjo ever wrote. People in those days were more robust when it came to slanging each other. The fact is that seven years later Paterson was prepared to go to bat for his old adversary Lawson in a doomed attempt to get him some justice from his publishers:

Henry Lawson was a man of remarkable insight in some things and of extraordinary simplicity in others. We were both looking for the same reef if you get what I mean; but I had done my

prospecting on horseback with my meals cooked
for me, while Lawson had done his prospecting on
foot and had had to cook for himself. Nobody
realised this better than Lawson, and one day he
suggested that we should write against each
other; he putting the bush from his point of view
and I putting it from mine.

'We ought to do pretty well out of it,' he said.
'We ought to be able to get in three or four sets of
verses each before they stop us.'

This suited me all right, for we were working
on space and the pay was very small—in fact,
I remember getting exactly thirteen and sixpence
for writing 'Clancy of the Overflow'—so we slam-
banged away at each other for weeks and weeks;
not until they stopped us, but until we ran out of
material. I think that Lawson put his case better
than I did but I had the better case, so that
honours (or dishonours) were fairly equal. An
undignified affair, but it was a case of 'root-hog-
or-die'.

To show how a poet can be without honour (or
profit) in his own country, I remember Lawson's
wife telling me that she was quite happy because
Henry was 'working' again.

'What's he working at,' I asked, 'prose or verse?'

'Oh no,' she said. 'I don't mean writing. I mean
working. He's gone back to his trade as a house
painter.'

And this was the man whose work was afterwards
translated into foreign languages!

BORDERLAND

(Henry Lawson)

I am back from up the country—very sorry that I
    went—
Seeking for the Southern poets' land whereon to
    pitch my tent;
I have lost a lot of idols, which were broken on the
    track—
Burnt a lot of fancy verses, and I am glad that I
    am back.
Further out may be the pleasant scenes of which
    our poets boast,
But I think the country's rather more inviting round
    the coast—
Anyway, I'll stay at present at a boarding house in
    town,
Drinking beers and lemon-squashes, taking baths
    and cooling down.

'Sunny Sandy plains!' Great Scot!—those burning
    wastes of barren soil and sand
With their everlasting fences stretching out across
    the land!
Desolation where the crow is! Desert where the eagle
    flies,
Paddocks where the luny bullock starts and stares
    with reddened eyes;
Where in clouds of dust enveloped, roasted bullock
    drivers creep
Slowly past the sun-dried shepherd dragged behind
    his crawling sheep.
Stunted peak of granite gleaming, glaring like a
    molten mass
Turned from some infernal furnace on a plain
    devoid of grass.

Miles and miles of thirsty gutters—strings of muddy
    waterholes
In the place of 'shining rivers' (walled by cliffs and
    forest boles).
'Ranges' of ridges, gullies, ridges! barren! where
    the madden'd flies—
Fiercer than the plagues of Egypt—swarm about
    your blighted eyes!
Bush! where there is no horizon! where the buried
    bushman sees
Nothing—Nothing! but the maddening sameness of
    the stunted trees!
Lonely—but where drought's eternal suffocating
    atmosphere—
Where the God forgotten hatter dreams of city-
    life and beer.

Treacherous tracks that trap the stranger, endless
    roads that gleam and glare.
Dark and evil looking gullies—hiding secrets here
    and there!
Dull, dumb flats and stony 'rises', where the bullocks
    sweat and bake,
And the sinister 'gohanna', and the lizard and the
    snake.
Land of day and night—no morning freshness, and
    no afternoon,
For the great, white sun in rising brings with him
    the heat of noon.
Dismal country for the exile, when the shades begin
    to fall
From the sad, heart-breaking sunset, to the new-
    chum worst of all.

Dreary land in rainy weather, with the endless
    clouds that drift
O'er the bushman like a blanket that the Lord
    will never lift—
Dismal land when it is raining—growl of floods
    and oh! the 'woosh'
Of the wind and rain together on the dark bed of the
    bush—
Ghastly fires in lonely humpies where the granite rocks
    are piled
On the rain-swept wildernesses that are the wildest
    of the wild.

Land where gaunt and haggard women live alone
    and work like men,
Till their husbands, gone a-droving, will return
    to them again;
Homes of men! if homes had ever such a God-
    forgotten place,
Where the wild selector's children fly before the
    stranger's face.
Home of tragedies applauded by the dingoes' dismal
    yell,
Heaven of the shanty-keeper—fitting fiend for such a
    hell—
And the wallaroos and wombats, and of course the
    'curlew's call'—
And the lone sundowner tramping ever onward thro'
    it all!

I am back from up the country—up the country where
    I went!
Seeking for the Southern poets' land whereon to pitch
    my tent;
I have left a lot of broken idols out along the track,
Burnt a lot of fancy verses—and I'm glad that I
    am back.

I believe the Southern poets' dream will not be
    realised
Till the plains are irrigated and the land is
    humanised.
I intend to stay at present—as I said before—in town
Drinking beer and lemon squashes—taking baths and
    cooling down.

> First published in the *Bulletin*,
> 7 July 1892. Later published as
> 'Up the Country' in the collection
> *In the Days When the World Was
> Wide*, 1900.

IN DEFENCE OF THE BUSH

(Banjo Paterson)

So you're back from up the country, Mister Lawson,
    where you went,
And you're cursing all the business in a bitter dis-
    content;
Well, we grieve to disappoint you, and it makes us
    sad to hear
That it wasn't cool and shady—and there wasn't whips
    of beer,
And the looney bullock snorted when you first came
    into view—
Well, you know it's not so often that he sees a swell
    like you;
And the roads were hot and dusty, and the plains
    were burnt and brown,
And no doubt you're better suited drinking lemon-
    squash in town.

Yet, perchance, if you should journey down the very
track you went
In a month or two at furthest, you would wonder
what it meant;
Where the sunbaked earth was gasping like a creature
in its pain
You would find the grasses waving like a field of
summer grain,
And the miles of thirsty gutters, blocked with sand
and choked with mud,
You would find them mighty rivers with a turbid,
sweeping flood.
For the rain and drought and sunshine make no
changes in the street,
In the sullen line of buildings and the ceaseless tramp
of feet;
But the bush has moods and changes, as the seasons
rise and fall,
And the men who know the bush-land—they are loyal
through it all.

•   •   •

But you found the bush was dismal and a land of
no delight—
Did you chance to hear a chorus in the shearers'
huts at night?
Did they 'rise up, William Riley' by the camp-fire's
cheery blaze?
Did they rise him as we rose him in the good old
droving days?
And the women of the homesteads and the men you
chanced to meet—
Were their faces sour and saddened like the 'faces
in the street?'
And the 'shy selector children'—were they better now
or worse
Than the little city urchins who would greet you with
a curse?

Is not such a life much better than the squalid street
    and square
Where the fallen women flaunt it in the fierce electric
    glare,
Where the sempstress plies her needle till her eyes
    are sore and red
In a filthy, dirty attic toiling on for daily bread?
Did you hear no sweeter voices in the music of the
    bush
Than the roar of trams and buses, and the war-whoop
    of 'the push?'
Did the magpies rouse your slumbers with their carol
    sweet and strange?
Did you hear the silver chiming of the bell-birds
    on the range?
But, perchance, the wild birds' music by your senses
    was despised,
For you say you'll stay in townships till the bush is
    civilized.
Would you make it a tea-garden, and on Sundays
    have a band
Where the 'blokes' might take their 'donahs', with
    a 'public' close at hand?
You had better stick to Sydney and make merry
    with the 'push',
For the bush will never suit you, and you'll never
    suit the bush.

Bulletin, 23 July 1892

In Answer to 'Banjo' and Otherwise

(Henry Lawson)

It was pleasant up the country, Mr Banjo, where you
    went,
For you sought the greener patches and you travelled
    like a gent,

And you curse the trams and buses and the turmoil
and the 'push',
Tho' you know the 'squalid city' needn't keep you from
the bush;
But we lately heard you singing of 'plains where the
shade is not',
And you mentioned it was dusty—'all is dry and
all is hot'.

True, the bush has 'moods and changes' and the
bushman hath them too—
For he's not a poet's dummy—he's a man the same
as you;
But his back is growing rounder slaving for the
'absentee'—
And his toiling wife is thinner than a country wife
should be.
For we noticed that the faces of the folks we chanced
to meet
Should have made a greater contrast to the faces in
the street;
And, in short, we think the bushman's being driven to
the wall.
And it's doubtful if his spirit will be *'loyal* thro' it
all'.

Tho' the bush has been romantic and it's nice to sing
about,
There's a lot of patriotism that the land could do
without—
Sort of BRITISH WORKMAN nonsense that shall perish
in the scorn
Of the drover who is driven and the shearer who is
shorn—

Of the struggling western farmers who have little
    time for rest,
And the ruin'd on selections in the squatter-ridden
    west—
Droving songs are very pretty, but they merit little
    thanks
From the people of a country which is ridden by the
    banks.

And the 'rise and fall of seasons' suits the rise and
    fall of rhyme,
But we know that western seasons do not run on
    'schedule time';
For the drought will go on drying while there's
    anything to dry,
Then it rains until you'd fancy it'd bleach the
    'sunny sky'—
Then it pelters out of reason, for the downpour day
    and night
Nearly sweeps the population to the Great Australian
    Bight.
It is up in Northern Queeensland that the 'seasons'
    do their best,
But it's doubtful if you ever saw a season in the
    west,
There are years without an autumn or a winter or a
    spring,
There are broiling Junes—and summers when it
    rains like anything.

In the bush my ears were opened to the singing of
    a bird,
But 'the carol of a magpie' was a thing I never
    heard.

Once the beggar raised my slumbers in a shanty,
    it is true.
But I only heard him asking, 'Who the blanky blank
    are you?'
And the bell-bird in the ranges—but his 'silver chime'
    is harsh
When it's heard beside the solo of the curlew in the
    marsh.

Yes, I heard the shearers singing 'William Riley' out
    of tune,
(Saw them fighting round a shanty on a Sunday
    afternoon.)
But the bushman isn't always 'trapping brumbies in
    the night',
Nor is he forever rising when 'the morn is fresh and
    bright'.
And he isn't always singing in the humpies on the
    run—
And the camp-fire's 'cheery blazes' are a trifle
    overdone;
We have grumbled with the bushmen round the fire
    on rainy days,
When the smoke would blind a bullock and there
    wasn't any blaze.
Save the blazes of our language, for we cursed the
    fire in turn
Till the atmosphere was heated and the wood began
    to burn.
Then we had to wring our blueys which were rotting
    in the swags,
And we saw the sugar leaking thro' the bottoms of the
    bags
And we couldn't raise a 'chorus', for the tooth-ache
    and the cramp.
While we spent the hours of darkness draining
    puddles round the camp.

Would you like to change with Clancy—go a'droving?
    tell us true,
For we rather think that Clancy would be glad to change
    with you.
And be something in the city; but 'twould give your muse
    a shock
To be losing time and money thro' the foot-rot in the
    flock,
And you wouldn't mind the beauties underneath the
    starry dome
If you had a wife and children and a lot of bills
    at home.

Did you ever guard the cattle when the night was
    inky-black,
And it rained, and icy water trickled gently down your
    back
Till your saddle-weary backbone fell a-aching to the
    roots
And you almost felt the croaking of the bull-frog
    in your boots—
Sit and shiver in the saddle, curse the restless
    stock and cough
Till a squatter's irate dummy cantered up to warn
    you off?
Did you fight the drought and 'pleuro' when the
    seasons were asleep—
Felling she oaks all the morning for a flock of hungry
    sheep
Drinking mud instead of water—climbing trees and
    lopping boughs
For the broken-hearted bullocks and the dry and dusty
    cows?

Did you think the bush was better 'in the good old
    droving days',
When the squatter ruled supremely as the king of
    western ways?

When you got a slip of paper for the little you
    could earn,
But were forced to take provisions from the station
    in return—
When you couldn't keep a chicken at your humpy
    on the run,
For the squatter wouldn't let you—and your work
    was never done;
When you had to leave the missus in the lonely
    hut forlorn
While you rose up 'Willy Riley' in the days ere you
    were born?

Ah! We read about the drovers and the shearers
    and the like
Till we wonder why such happy and romantic fellows
    'strike'.

Don't you fancy that the poets better give the bush
    a rest
Ere they raise a just rebellion in the over-written
    West?
Where the simple-minded bushman gets a meal and
    bed and rum
Just by riding round reporting phantom flocks that
    never come;
Where the scalper—never troubled by the
    'war-whoop of the push'—
Has a quiet little billet—breeding rabbits in the
    bush;
Where the idle shanty-keeper never fails to make a
    'draw'.
And the dummy gets his tucker thro' provisions in the
    law;
Where the labour-agitator—when the shearers rise
    in might—
Makes his money sacrificing all his substance for
    The Right:

Where the squatter makes his fortune and the
    seasons 'rise' and 'fall',
And the poor and honest bushman has to suffer
    for it all,
Where the drovers and the shearers and the bushmen
    and the rest
Never reach the Eldorado of the poets of the West.

And you think the bush is purer and that life is
    better there,
But it doesn't seem to pay you like 'the squalid street
    and square'.
Pray inform us, 'Mr. Banjo', where you read, in
    prose or verse,
Of the awful 'city urchin' who would greet you with
    a curse.
There are golden hearts in gutters, tho' their owners
    lack the fat,
And we'll back a teamster's offspring to outswear
    a city brat;
Do you think we're never jolly where the trams and
    buses rage?
Did you hear the gods in chorus when 'Ri-Tooral'
    held the stage?
Did you catch a ring of sorrow in the city urchin's
    voice
When he yelled for 'Billy Elton', when he thumped
    the floor for Royce?
Do the bushmen, down on pleasure, miss the
    everlasting stars
When they drink and flirt and so on in the glow
    of private bars?

What care you if fallen women 'flaunt'! God help
    'em—let 'em flaunt
And if the seamstress seems to haunt you—to what
    purpose does she haunt?

You're down on 'trams and buses', or 'the roar' of
    'em, you said,
And the 'filthy, dirty attic' where you never toiled
    for bread.
(And about that self-same attic—tell us, Banjo, where
    you've been?
For the striving needle-woman mostly keeps her
    attic clean.)
But you'll find it very jolly with the cuff-and-collar
    push.
And the city seems to suit you, while you rave about
    the bush.

P.S.
You'll admit that 'up-the-country', more especially
    in the drought,
Isn't quite the Eldorado that the poets rave
    about.
Yet at times we long to gallop where the reckless
    bushman rides
In the wake of frightened brumbies that are fleeing
    for their hides:
Long to feel the saddle tremble once again between
    our knees
And to hear the stock-whips rattle just like rifles
    in the trees!
Long to feel the bridle-leather tugging strongly in
    our hand
And to feel once more a little like 'a native of the
    land'.
And the ring of bitter feelings in the jingling of
    our rhymes
Isn't suited to the country or the spirit of our times.

Let us go together droving, and returning, if we
    live,
Try to understand each other while we liquor up
    the 'div'.

> First published in the *Bulletin*,
> 6 August 1892. Later published as
> 'The City Bushmen' in the collection
> *In the Days When the World Was
> Wide*, 1900.

An Answer to Various Bards

(Banjo Paterson)

Well, I've waited mighty patient while they all came
    rolling in,
Mister Lawson, Mister Dyson, and the others of
    their kin,
With their dreadful, dismal stories of the Over-lander's
    camp,
How his fire is always smoky, and his boots are always
    damp;
And they paint it so terrific it would fill one's soul
    with gloom—
But you know they're fond of writing about 'corpses'
    and 'the tomb'.
So, before they curse the bushland, they should let
    their fancy range,
And take something for their livers, and be cheerful
    for a change.

Now, for instance, Mr. Lawson—well, of course, we
    almost cried
At the sorrowful description how his 'little 'Arvie' died,

And we lachrymosed in silence when 'His Father's
    Mate' was slain;
Then he went and killed the father, and we had to
    weep again.
Ben Duggan and Jack Denver, too, he caused them
    to expire,
After which he cooked the gander of Jack Dunn, of
    Nevertire;
And, no doubt, the bush *is* wretched if you judge it by
    the groan
Of the sad and soulful poet with a graveyard of his
    own.

And he spoke in terms prophetic of a revolution's
    heat,
When the world should hear the clamour of those
    people in the street;
But the shearer chaps who start it—why, he rounds
    on them in blame,
And he calls 'em 'agitators who are living on the
    game'.
But I 'over-write' the bushmen! Well, I own without
    a doubt
That I always see a hero in the 'man from furthest
    out'.
I could never contemplate him through an atmosphere
    of gloom,
And a bushman never struck me as a subject for 'the
    tomb'.

If it ain't all 'golden sunshine' where the 'wattle
    branches wave',
Well, it ain't all damp and dismal, and it ain't all
    'lonely grave'.

And, of course, there's no denying that the bush-
man's life is rough,
But a man can easy stand it if he's built of sterling
stuff;
Though it's seldom that the drover gets a bed of
eiderdown,
Yet the man who's born a bushman, he gets mighty
sick of town,
For he's jotting down the figures, and he's adding
up the bills
While his heart is simply aching for a sight of
Southern hills.

Then he hears a wool-team passing with a rumble
and a lurch,
And, although the work is pressing, yet it brings
him off his perch.
For it stirs him like a message from his station
friends afar
And he seems to sniff the ranges in the scent of wool
and tar;
And it takes him back in fancy, half in laughter, half
in tears,
To a sound of other voices and a thought of other
years,
When the woolshed rang with bustle from the dawning
of the day,
And the shear-blades were a-clicking to the cry of
'Wool away!'

Then his face was somewhat browner, and his frame
was firmer set—
And he feels his flabby muscles with a feeling of
regret.
But the wool-team slowly passes, and his eyes go
sadly back
To the dusty little table and the papers in the rack,

And his thoughts go to the terrace where his sickly
    children squall,
And he thinks there's something healthy in the bush-
    life after all.
But we'll go no more a-droving in the wind or in the
    sun,
For our fathers' hearts have failed us, and the
    droving days are done.

There's a nasty dash of danger where the long-horned
    bullock wheels,
And we like to live in comfort and to get our reg'lar
    meals.
For to hang around the townships suits us better,
    you'll agree,
And a job at washing bottles is the job for such as
    we.
Let us herd into the cities, let us crush and crowd
    and push
Till we lose the love of roving, and we learn to hate
    the bush;
And we'll turn our aspirations to a city life and
    beer,
And we'll slip across to England—it's a nicer place
    than here;

For there's not much risk of hardship where all
    comforts are in store,
And the theatres are in plenty, and the pubs are
    more and more.
But that ends it, Mr. Lawson, and it's time to say
    good-bye,
So we must agree to differ in all friendship, you
    and I.

Yes, we'll work our own salvation with the stoutest
    hearts we may,
And if fortune only favours we will take the road
    some day,
And go droving down the river 'neath the sunshine
    and the stars,
And then return to Sydney and vermilionize the
    bars.

Bulletin, 1 October 1892

The Comic Side

... 'Murder! Bloody Murder!' yelled the man from Ironbark ...

The historian of the *Bulletin*, Patricia Rolfe, records with regret that comic verse as a form of journalism now seems dead, although its counterpart—cartooning—is alive and well. The late Victorian age, where Banjo Paterson made his name, was the high era of light comic verse, trippingly dashed off without pretension, and Paterson was the best of the pack.

In the new century the *Bulletin* was to go into rapid decline and the grey world of the rest of the Australian press had little place for flippancy, preferring the fake sentimentalisms of C.J. Dennis. Paterson's later light verse, published in the *Sydney Sportsman* in the twenties, was something of an anachronism.

THE MAN FROM IRONBARK

It was the man from Ironbark who struck the
    Sydney town,
He wandered over street and park, he wandered
    up and down.
He loitered here, he loitered there, till he was like
    to drop,
Until at last in sheer despair he sought a barber's
    shop.
''Ere! shave my beard and whiskers off, I'll be a
    man of mark,
I'll go and do the Sydney toff up home in Iron-
    bark.'

The barber man was small and flash, as barbers
    mostly are,
He wore a strike-your-fancy sash, he smoked a huge
    cigar:
He was a humorist of note and keen at repartee,
He laid the odds and kept a 'tote', whatever that
    may be.
And when he saw our friend arrive, he whispered
    'Here's a lark!
Just watch me catch him all alive this man from
    Ironbark.'

There were some gilded youths that sat along the
    barber's wall,
Their eyes were dull, their heads were flat, they
    had no brains at all;
To them the barber passed the wink, his dexter
    eyelid shut,
'I'll make this bloomin' yokel think his bloomin'
    throat is cut.'

And as he soaped and rubbed it in he made a rude
    remark:
'I s'pose the flats is pretty green up there in Iron-
    bark.'

A grunt was all reply he got; he shaved the bush-
    man's chin,
Then made the water boiling hot and dipped the
    razor in.
He raised his hand, his brow grew black, he paused
    awhile to gloat,
Then slashed the red-hot razor-back across his
    victim's throat;
Upon the newly-shaven skin it made a livid mark—
No doubt it fairly took him in— the man from Iron-
    bark.

He fetched a wild up-country yell might wake the
    dead to hear,
And though his throat, he knew full well, was cut
    from ear to ear,
He struggled gamely to his feet, and faced the
    murderous foe:
'You've done for me! you dog, I'm beat! one hit
    before I go!
I only wish I had a knife, you blessed murdering
    shark!
But you'll remember all your life the man from
    Ironbark.'

He lifted up his hairy paw, with one tremendous
    clout
He landed on the barber's jaw, and knocked the
    barber out.
He set to work with tooth and nail, he made the
    place a wreck;
He grabbed the nearest gilded youth, and tried to
    break his neck.

And all the while his throat he held to save his
    vital spark,
And 'Murder! Bloody Murder!' yelled the man
    from Ironbark.

A peeler man who heard the din came in to see
    the show;
He tried to run the bushman in, but he refused
    to go.
And when at last the barber spoke, and said "Twas
    all in fun—
'Twas just a little harmless joke, a trifle overdone.'
'A joke!' he cried, 'By George, that's fine; a lively
    sort of lark;
I'd like to catch that murdering swine some night
    in Ironbark.'

And now while round the shearing-floor the listen-
    ing shearers gape,
He tells the story o'er and o'er, and brags of his
    escape.
'Them barber chaps what keeps a tote, by George,
    I've had enough,
One tried to cut my bloomin' throat, but thank
    the Lord it's tough.'
And whether he's believed or no, there's one thing
    to remark,
That flowing beards are all the go way up in Iron-
    bark.

Bulletin, 17 December 1892

HOW M'GINNIS WENT MISSING

Let us cease our idle chatter,
    Let the tears bedew our cheek,
For a man from Tallangatta
    Has been missing for a week.

Where the roaring flooded Murray
  Covered all the lower land,
There he started in a hurry,
  With a bottle in his hand.

And his fate is hid for ever,
  But the public seem to think
That he slumbered by the river,
  'Neath the influence of drink.

And they scarcely seem to wonder
  That the river, wide and deep,
Never woke him with its thunder,
  Never stirred him in his sleep.

As the crashing logs came sweeping,
  And their tumult filled the air,
Then M'Ginnis murmured, sleeping,
  ''Tis a wake in ould Kildare.'

So the river rose and found him
  Sleeping softly by the stream,
And the cruel waters drowned him
  Ere he wakened from his dream.

And the blossom-tufted wattle,
  Blooming brightly on the lea,
Saw M'Ginnis and the bottle
  Going drifting out to sea.

Bulletin, 21 December 1889

JOHNSON'S ANTIDOTE

Down along the Snakebite River, where the over-
    landers camp,
Where the serpents are in millions, all of the most
    deadly stamp;
Where the station-cook in terror, nearly every time
    he bakes,
Mixes up among the doughboys half a dozen poison-
    snakes:
Where the wily free-selector walks in armour-plated
    pants,
And defies the stings of scorpions, and the bites of
    bull-dog ants:
Where the adder and the viper tear each other by
    the throat—
There it was that William Johnson sought his
    snakebite antidote.

Johnson was a free-selector, and his brain went
    rather queer,
For the constant sight of serpents filled him with
    a deadly fear;
So he tramped his free-selection, morning, after-
    noon, and night,
Seeking for some great specific that would cure the
    serpent's bite.
Till King Billy, of the Mooki, chieftain of the flour-
    bag head,
Told him, 'Spos'n snake bite pfeller, pfeller mostly
    drop down dead;
Spos'n snake bite old goanna, then you watch a
    while you see
Old goanna cure himself with eating little pfeller
    tree.'

'That's the cure,' said William Johnson, 'point
me out this plant sublime,'
But King Billy, feeling lazy, said he'd go another
time.
Thus it came to pass that Johnson, having got the
tale by rote,
Followed every stray goanna seeking for the anti-
dote.

       •   •   •

Loafing once beside the river, while he thought his
heart would break,
There he saw a big goanna fighting with a tiger-
snake.
In and out they rolled and wriggled, bit each other,
heart and soul,
Till the valiant old goanna swallowed his opponent
whole.
Breathless, Johnson sat and watched him, saw him
struggle up the bank,
Saw him nibbling at the branches of some bushes,
green and rank;
Saw him, happy and contented, lick his lips, as off
he crept,
While the bulging of his stomach showed where
his opponent slept.
Then a cheer of exultation burst aloud from
Johnson's throat;
'Luck at last,' said he, 'I've struck it! 'tis the
famous antidote.

'Here it is, the Grand Elixir, greatest blessing ever
known—
Twenty thousand men in India die each year of
snakes alone;
Think of all the foreign nations, negro, chow, and
blackamoor,

Saved from sudden expiration by my wondrous
    snakebite cure.
It will bring me fame and fortune! In the happy
    days to be
Men of every clime and nation will be round to gaze
    on me—
Scientific men in thousands, men of mark and men
    of note,
Rushing down the Mooki River, after Johnson's
    antidote.
It will cure *delirium tremens* when the patient's
    eyeballs stare
At imaginary spiders, snakes which really are not
    there.
When he thinks he sees them wriggle, when he
    thinks he sees them bloat,
It will cure him just to think of Johnson's Snake-
    bite Antidote.'

Then he rushed to the museum, found a scientific
    man—
'Trot me out a deadly serpent, just the deadliest
    you can;
I intend to let him bite me, all the risk I will
    endure,
Just to prove the sterling value of my wondrous
    snakebite cure.
Even though an adder bit me, back to life again
    I'd float;
Snakes are out of date, I tell you, since I've found
    the antidote.'

Said the scientific person, 'If you really want to
    die,
Go ahead—but, if you're doubtful, let your sheep-
    dog have a try.

Get a pair of dogs and try it, let the snake give
   both a nip;
Give your dog the snakebite mixture, let the other
   fellow rip;
If he dies and yours survives him, then it proves the
   thing is good.
Will you fetch your dog and try it?' Johnson rather
   thought he would.
So he went and fetched his canine, hauled him
   forward by the throat.
'Stump, old man,' says he, 'we'll show them we've
   the genwine antidote.'

Both the dogs were duly loaded with the poison-
   gland's contents;
Johnson gave his dog the mixture, then sat down
   to wait events.
'Mark,' he said, 'in twenty minutes Stump'll be
   a-rushing round,
While the other wretched creature lies a corpse
   upon the ground.'
But, alas for William Johnson! ere they'd watched
   a half-hour's spell
Stumpy was as dead as mutton, t'other dog was
   live and well.
And the scientific person hurried off with utmost
   speed,
Tested Johnson's drug and found it was a deadly
   poison-weed;
Half a tumbler killed an emu, half a spoonful killed
   a goat—
All the snakes on earth were harmless to that awful
   antidote.

•   •   •

Down along the Mooki River, on the overlanders'
   camp,
Where the serpents are in millions, all of the most
   deadly stamp,

Wanders, daily, William Johnson, down among
    those poisonous hordes,
Shooting every stray goanna, calls them 'black
    and yaller frauds'.
And King Billy, of the Mooki, cadging for the cast-
    off coat,
Somehow seems to dodge the subject of the snake-
    bite antidote.

Bulletin, 26 January 1895

A Bush Christening

On the outer Barcoo where the churches are few,
    And men of religion are scanty,
On a road never cross'd 'cept by folk that are lost
    One Michael Magee had a shanty.

Now this Mike was the dad of a ten-year-old lad,
    Plump, healthy, and stoutly conditioned;
He was strong as the best, but poor Mike had no
    rest
    For the youngster had never been christened.

And his wife used to cry, 'If the darlin' should die
    Saint Peter would not recognize him.'
But by luck he survived till a preacher arrived,
    Who agreed straightaway to baptize him.

Now the artful young rogue, while they held their
    collogue,
    With his ear to the keyhole was listenin';
And he muttered in fright, while his features turned
    white,
    'What the divil and all is this christenin'?'

He was none of your dolts—he had seen them brand
    colts,
    And it seemed to his small understanding,
If the man in the frock made him one of the flock,
    It must mean something very like branding.

So away with a rush he set off for the bush,
    While the tears in his eyelids they glistened—
' 'Tis outrageous,' says he, 'to brand youngsters
    like me;
    I'll be dashed if I'll stop to be christened!'

Like a young native dog he ran into a log,
    And his father with language uncivil,
Never heeding the 'praste', cried aloud in his
    haste
    'Come out and be christened, you divil!'

But he lay there as snug as a bug in a rug,
    And his parents in vain might reprove him,
Till his reverence spoke (he was fond of a joke)
    'I've a notion,' says he, 'that'll move him.'

'Poke a stick up the log, give the spalpeen a prog;
    Poke him aisy—don't hurt him or maim him;
'Tis not long that he'll stand, I've the water at hand,
    As he rushes out this end I'll name him.

'Here he comes, and for shame! ye've forgotten
    the name—
    Is it Patsy or Michael or Dinnis?'
Here the youngster ran out, and the priest gave a
    shout—
    'Take your chance, anyhow, wid "Maginnis"!'

As the howling young cub ran away to the scrub
   Where he knew that pursuit would be risky,
The priest, as he fled, flung a flask at his head
   That was labelled 'Maginnis's Whisky!'

Now Maginnis Magee has been made a J.P.,
   And the one thing he hates more than sin is
To be asked by the folk, who have heard of the joke,
   How he came to be christened Maginnis!

Bulletin, 16 December 1893

MULGA BILL'S BICYCLE

'Twas Mulga Bill, from Eaglehawk, that caught the
   cycling craze;
He turned away the good old horse that served him
   many days;
He dressed himself in cycling clothes, resplendent to
   be seen;
He hurried off to town and bought a shining new
   machine;
And as he wheeled it through the door, with air
   of lordly pride,
The grinning shop assistant said, 'Excuse me, can
   you ride?'

'See here, young man,' said Mulga Bill, 'from Walgett
   to the sea,
From Conroy's Gap to Castlereagh, there's none
   can ride like me.
I'm good all round at everything, as everybody
   knows,
Although I'm not the one to talk—I hate a man
   that blows.

'But riding is my special gift, my chiefest, sole
     delight;
Just ask a wild duck can it swim, a wild cat can it
     fight.
There's nothing clothed in hair or hide, or built of
     flesh or steel
There's nothing walks or jumps, or runs, on axle,
     hoof, or wheel,
But what I'll sit, while hide will hold and girths
     and straps are tight;
I'll ride this here two-wheeled concern right
     straight away at sight.'

'Twas Mulga Bill, from Eaglehawk, that sought his
     own abode,
That perched above the Dead Man's Creek, beside
     the mountain road.
He turned the cycle down the hill and mounted for
     the fray,
But ere he'd gone a dozen yards it bolted clean
     away.
It left the track, and through the trees, just like a
     silver streak,
It whistled down the awful slope towards the Dead
     Man's Creek.

It shaved a stump by half an inch, it dodged a big
     white-box:
The very wallaroos in fright went scrambling up
     the rocks,
The wombats hiding in their caves dug deeper
     underground,
But Mulga Bill, as white as chalk, sat tight to every
     bound.

It struck a stone and gave a spring that cleared a
    fallen tree,
It raced beside a precipice as close as close could
     be;
And then, as Mulga Bill let out one last despairing
    shriek,
It made a leap of twenty feet into the Dead Man's
    Creek.

'Twas Mulga Bill, from Eaglehawk, that slowly
    swam ashore:
He said, 'I've had some narrer shaves and lively
    rides before;
I've rode a wild bull round a yard to win a five-
    pound bet,
But this was sure the derndest ride that I've
    encountered yet.
I'll give that two-wheeled outlaw best; it's shaken
    all my nerve
To feel it whistle through the air and plunge and
    buck and swerve.
It's safe at rest in Dead Man's Creek—we'll leave it
    lying still;
A horse's back is good enough henceforth for Mulga
    Bill.'

> First published in the *Sydney Mail*,
> 25 July 1896. This version published
> in *Rio Grande's Last Race*, 1902.

IT's GRAND

It's grand to be a squatter
  And sit upon a post,
And watch your little ewes and lambs
  A-giving up the ghost.

It's grand to be a 'cockie'
  With wife and kids to keep,
And find an all-wise Providence
  Has mustered all your sheep.

It's grand to be a Western man,
  With shovel in your hand,
To dig your little homestead out
  From underneath the sand.

It's grand to be a shearer
  Along the Darling-side,
And pluck the wool from stinking sheep
  That some days since have died.

It's grand to be a rabbit
  And breed till all is blue,
And then to die in heaps because
  There's nothing left to chew.

It's grand to be a Minister
  And travel like a swell,
And tell the Central District folk
  To go to—Inverell.

It's grand to be a socialist
  And lead the bold array
That marches to prosperity
  At seven bob a day.

It's grand to be an unemployed
  And lie in the Domain,
And wake up every second day—
  And go to sleep again.

It's grand to borrow English tin
　To pay for wharves and docks,
And then to find it isn't in
　The little money-box.

It's grand to be a democrat
　And toady to the mob,
For fear that if you told the truth
　They'd hunt you from your job.

It's grand to be a lot of things
　In this fair Southern land,
But if the Lord would send us rain,
　That would, indeed, be grand!

Bulletin, 25 May 1902

THE CITY OF DREADFUL THIRST

The stranger came from Narromine and made his
　little joke;
'They say we folks in Narromine are narrow-minded
　folk;
But all the smartest men down here are puzzled to
　define
A kind of new phenomenon that came to Narromine.

'Last summer up in Narromine 'twas gettin' rather
　warm—
Two hundred in the water-bag, and lookin' like a
　storm—
We all were in the private bar, the coolest place in
　town,
When out across the stretch of plain a cloud came
　rollin' down.

'We don't respect the clouds up there, they fill us
    with disgust,
They mostly bring a Bogan shower—three rain-drops
    and some dust;
But each man, simultaneous-like, to each man said,
    'I think
That cloud suggests it's up to us to have another
    drink!'

'There's clouds of rain and clouds of dust—we'd heard
    of them before,
And sometimes in the daily press we read of 'clouds
    of war':
But—if this ain't the Gospel truth I hope that I may
    burst—
That cloud that came to Narromine was just a cloud
    of thirst.

'It wasn't like a common cloud, 'twas more a sort
    of haze;
It settled down about the streets, and stopped for days
    and days;
And not a drop of dew could fall, and not a sunbeam
    shine
To pierce that dismal sort of mist that hung on
    Narromine.

'Oh, Lord! we had a dreadful time beneath that cloud
    of thirst!
We all chucked-up our daily work and went upon
    the burst.
The very blacks about the town, that used to cadge
    for grub,
They made an organized attack and tried to loot the
    pub.

'We couldn't leave the private bar no matter how
    we tried;
Shearers and squatters, union-men and blacklegs
    side by side
Were drinkin' there and dursn't move, for each was
    sure, he said,
Before he'd get a half-a-mile the thirst would strike
    him dead!

'We drank until the drink gave out; we searched from
    room to room,
And round the pub, like drunken ghosts, went
    howling through the gloom.
The shearers found some kerosene and settled down
    again,
But all the squatter chaps and I, we staggered to
    the train.

'And once outside the cloud of thirst we felt as right
    as pie,
But while we stopped about the town we had to drink
    or die.
I hear to-day it's safe enough; I'm going back to
    work
Because they say the cloud of thirst has shifted on
    to Bourke.

'But when you see those clouds about—like this one
    over here—
All white and frothy at the top, just like a pint of
    beer,
It's time to go and have a drink, for if that cloud
    should burst
You'd find the drink would all be gone, for that's a
    cloud of thirst!'

•   •   •

We stood the man from Narromine a pint of half-
and-half;
He drank it off without a gasp in one tremendous
quaff;
'I joined some friends last night,' he said, 'in what
they called a spree;
But after Narromine 'twas just a holiday to me.'

And now beyond the Western Range, where sunset
skies are red,
And clouds of dust, and clouds of thirst, go drifting
overhead,
The railway train is taking back, along the Western
Line.
That narrow-minded person on his road to
Narromine.

Bulletin, 9 December 1899

WHEN DACEY RODE THE MULE

'Twas to a small, up-country town,
  When we were boys at school,
There came a circus with a clown,
  Likewise a bucking mule.
The clown announced a scheme they had
  Spectators for to bring—
They'd give a crown to any lad
  Who'd ride him round the ring.

  And, gentle reader, do not scoff
    Nor think a man a fool—
  To buck a porous-plaster off
    Was pastime to that mule.

The boys got on; he bucked like sin;
  He threw them in the dirt.
What time the clown would raise a grin
  By asking, 'Are you hurt?'

But Johnny Dacey came one night,
   The crack of all the school;
Said he, 'I'll win the crown all right;
   Bring in your bucking mule.'

      The elephant went off his trunk,
         The monkey played the fool,
      And all the band got blazing drunk
         When Dacey rode the mule.

But soon there rose a galling shout
   Of laughter, for the clown
From somewhere in his pants drew out
   A little paper crown.
He placed the crown on Dacey's head
   While Dacey looked a fool;
'Now, there's your crown, my lad,' he said,
   'For riding of the mule!'

      The band struck up with 'Killaloe',
         And 'Rule Britannia, Rule',
      And 'Young Man from the Country', too,
         When Dacey rode the mule.

Then Dacey, in a furious rage,
   For vengeance on the show
Ascended to the monkeys' cage
   And let the monkeys go;

The blue-tailed ape and chimpanzee
   He turned abroad to roam;
Good faith! It was a sight to see
   The people step for home.

For big baboons with canine snout
  Are spiteful, as a rule—
The people didn't sit it out,
  When Dacey rode the mule.

And from the beasts he let escape,
  The bushman all declare,
Were born some creatures partly ape
  And partly native-bear.
They're rather few and far between,
  The race is nearly spent;
But some of them may still be seen
  In Sydney Parliament.

And when those legislators fight,
  And drink, and act the fool,
Just blame it on that torrid night
  When Dacey rode the mule.

Bulletin, 8 July 1893

ANY OTHER TIME (A BALLAD OF GOOD EXCUSES: 'THE ROAD TO HELL IS PAVED WITH GOOD INTENTIONS')

All of us play our very best game
  Any other time;
Golf or billiards, it's all the same
  Any other time.
Lose a match and you always say:
'Just my luck, I was "off" to-day;
I could have beaten him quite half way
  Any other time'.

After a fiver you ought to go
  Any other time.
Every man that you ask says, 'Oh,
  Any other time!

Lend you a fiver, I'd lend you two,
But I'm overdrawn and my bills are due.
Wish you'd ask me—now mind you do—
    Any other time'.

Fellows will ask you out to dine
    Any other time.
'Not to-night, for I'm short of wine',
    Any other time!
'Not to-morrow, the cook's on strike,
Not next day—I'll be out on the bike—
Just drop in whenever you like,
    Any other time'.

All mankind will be better men
    Any other time.
Regular upright characters then,
    Any other time.
They mean to reform as the years go by,
But still they gamble and drink and lie;
When it comes to the end they'd want to die
    Any other time!

First published in *Rio Grande's Last Race*, 1902. This version appeared in the *Sydney Sportsman*, 26 December 1923.

Last Words

. . . I watched Pardon's progress—watched him lying behind the leaders as they went out of sight behind the stringy-bark scrub; watched them come into sight again, with Pardon still lying third; and then the crowning moment as he drew away in the straight and won comfortably. Greater still, the delirious joy when he led the field all the way in the second heat, so that there was no need for a third.

Master Andrew Barton Paterson,
aged 8, at his first race meeting.

In February–March 1939, Paterson published his reminiscences in the *Sydney Morning Herald*. They were not an attempt at a full autobiography, rather a set of gentle memories. There was nothing of men dying in battle in the Boer war, but rather a lot of what a lonely and keenly observant child saw growing up in the bush. The reminiscences end at Coodra Vale, scene of his failure as a Murrumbidgee squatter, which he characteristically treated with gentle irony. There is a freshness about his memories that vividly evokes a lost rural society. He remembers not only Pardon's victory, but also the taste of the ginger beer that day.

In one of the series he is perhaps making amends for being economical with the truth a long time before, when he had defended fellow balladist Breaker Morant, executed by the British during the Boer War. At the time, Morant had been elevated by the Australian public to the status of a martyr. Forty years on, an older Paterson felt he could be rather more frank about the Breaker's character. But these are the only hard words. In the end, the articles are the reminiscences of a happy and generous man.

'BANJO' PATERSON TELLS HIS OWN STORY

Some seventy years ago, two Scotsmen, John and Andrew Paterson, were 'squatting' at a station called Buckenbah, somewhere near the town of Obley, in the western district of New South Wales. This place was held on lease from the Crown at a few pence per acre and was worth no more. It was dingo-infested, unfenced country where the sheep had to be shepherded and the cattle, as the blackboys said, could go 'longa bush' and wander afield until they got into somebody else's meat cask or could be mustered and driven away by enterprising people who adopted this cheap method of stocking-up. In these surroundings, I, the immature verse-writer, son of Andrew Paterson, had my first taste of bush life.

My father was a lowland Scot, a son of a captain in the old East India Company's service, though his family before him had for generations farmed their own properties in Lanarkshire. One of my father's forebears was John Paterson of Lochlyoch, who founded the breed of Clydesdale horses by importing a black Flemish stallion called Robin.

Robin was to the Clydesdale breed what Eclipse was to the thoroughbred, as may be seen in the Clydesdale stud book. There was also a further connection with horses in that my grandfather, going out to India to seek his fortune, joined up with John Company's army, in which his original rank was that of a roughrider. He rode the rough horses so well that he afterwards obtained his commission; and it is something of a coincidence that in the Great War more than a hundred years afterwards, I, his grandson, was given a command as major in a roughriding unit. That, and my early experiences as a small shepherd, may account for whatever of accuracy there may be in my verified descriptions of bush life and of horses.

An ancestor whose talents I, unfortunately, failed to inherit was William Paterson, who founded the Bank of England. He is described in the Encyclopaedia as a 'Scotch adventurer', and 'adventurer' is right; for not satisfied with starting the Bank of England on its primrose path, he aspired to follow the example of Clive and Hastings and found a sort of Scottish East India Company at Darien on the Isthmus of Panama. Had his Bank of England luck stuck to him he might have been another Cecil Rhodes, for the Scotchmen poured their money into the venture; but the malaria and the mosquitoes beat him and he returned to Scotland to face his countrymen who had lost their money. Instead of upbraiding him they subscribed £10 000 to put him on his feet again!

Of my father I saw little, for he was mostly away pioneering in Queensland. There he had a skirmish with blacks, during which his cousin, James Paterson, had his spectacles knocked off his nose by the tip of a boomerang; he tried to take sheep out to some new place, but was caught on flooded country between two rivers, and had to shear them on a sandhill; and finally he had to get out of Queensland—just another of the many pioneers who unsuccessfully threw dice with fate. I never knew the name of his place in Queensland, but I understand it adjoined Lammermuir, the station described in *Christison of Lammermuir*, probably the second best tale ever told of bush life, Jeannie Gunn's *We of the Never-Never* being the best.

However, to meet losses in Queensland, Buckenbah had to go, and we moved to Illalong, a station in the southern part of New South Wales. Here we were on a main road between Sydney and Melbourne, with the Lambing Flat diggings, now called Young, only a day's ride away. It was an unlucky place—enough to break anyone's heart—for the Free Selection Act had just been passed and the selectors, droves of them, all seemed to pick on us, as there were creeks everywhere which solved for them the water problem.

But all these troubles meant nothing to me, a boy of six. There were swimming pools in the creek 10 feet deep and half a mile long, horses to ride, and the tides of life surged round us. The gold escort from Lambing Flat, too, came by twice a week, with a mounted trooper riding in front with his rifle at the ready and another armed trooper on the box with the coachman. I used to hope that the escort would be 'stuck up' outside our place so that I might see something worthwhile, but what with the new settlers and the scores of bullock teams taking loading out to the back country, no bushranger stood half a chance of making a getaway unseen.

The roads were quite unmade, and when one track got so cut up that a wagon would sink down to the axles, the bullocks would try a new track. Thus the highway became a labyrinth of tracks, half a mile wide, with here and there an excavation where a wagon had been dug out; and when, as often happened, a wagon got stuck in the bed of the creek, they would hitch two teams of bullocks to it and then (as one of the bullockies said) either the wagon or the bed of the creek had to come.

I was not encouraged to go anywhere near the bullockies, who were supposed to be up to stratagems and spoils, especially in the way of stealing horses; but a lonely child will go anywhere for company, and I found that they travelled with their families, dogs and sometimes even fowls. These latter gentry, after fossicking about the camp for worms and grasshoppers, would hop up into the wagon as soon as the bullocks were yoked; making for their crate, where a little food awaited them. They hurried, too!

I found that these teamsters were like Bracken's hero— 'not understood'. Hard as it may be to believe, they were really fond of their bullocks, and only took the whip to shirkers. One of them gave me a demonstration with a bullock-whip, cutting great furrows in the bark of a white gum tree. When I said that it was no wonder the bullocks pulled, he remarked feelingly, 'Sonny, if I done that to them bullocks, I'd want shooting. Every bullock knows his name, and when I speak to him he's into the yoke. I'd look well knocking 'em about with a hundred miles to go and them not gettin' a full feed once a week. Many a night I've dug up a panel of a squatter's paddock and slipped 'em in, and I've been back there before daylight to slip 'em out and put the panel up again. So long as they'll stick to me, I'll stick to them.'

Which somehow recalls the story of the bullock driver, who was asked to join up for the South African war, and was told that he need not fight as he would be more useful driving bullocks.

'Not me!' he said. 'I'd sooner fight. If there come any trouble, all you coves could run away, but I'd have to stop with the bullocks, and get caught!'

By this time I had learnt to ride, and to get me away it was decided that I should ride four miles to school every day in Binalong, a two-pub town famous for the fact that the bushranger Gilbert was buried in the police station paddock. Here I sat on a hard wooden form alongside some juvenile relatives of Gilbert.

Carlyle in his *Sartor Resartus* speaks of his hero Diogenes Teudelsdrock as being educated at the Academy of Hinterschlag ('stern whackers'), and there was plenty of Hinterschlag at this little bush school in Binalong. The master, Moore by name, had to meet emergencies of one sort or another every day, and he met them like a Napoleon. Spare, gaunt, and Irish by descent, he ran to gamecocks and kangaroo dogs in his private moments. It was nothing unusual for his flock to go out with him in the long summer afternoons to watch a course after a kangaroo, and the elite of the school, the poundkeeper's sop and the blacksmith's boy, would be allowed as a favour to stop after school and watch a 'go-in' between two cocks without the steel spurs, as part of their training for more serious business.

One day the sergeant of police from Yass, in plain clothes, drove up to the door of the school in a natty little trap with a pair of ponies. We jumped to the conclusion that he had heard of this cock fighting business, and we expected (and hoped) to see the schoolmaster led away like Eugene Aram with gyves upon his wrists. While the sergeant was inside with the teacher we children swarmed all over his buggy, and there in a neat lattice-lined box under the seat we found a gamecock, clipped and looking for fight!

The gamecock was rather surprised to see us in charge of his caravan, but not nearly so astonished as we were to see *him*. It was our—or at any rate, my—first introduction to the ways of the world and to those who go about in sheep's clothing, but are inwardly ravening wolves.

Apart from his sporting proclivities there was little fault to find with our teacher. Poor man, he was almost daily confronted by irate mothers, real rough sorts, whose children he had whipped, and who threatened to bring 'the old man' down to deal with him if it ever happened again.

My first introduction to the racing business came about in this way. It was a New Year's day and a general holiday. My father was away, and the station roustabout, having filled the water-barrel, cut the wood and fed the fowls, was free to go to the Bogolong races, some eight miles away. He suggested that I should go with him, and my mother agreed, though I would not have had a hundred-to-one chance of getting leave from my father. Picture us then, a youth of 18 and a boy of eight setting out to take part in the sport of kings!

Bogolong (now called Bookham) was a township on the main southern road, and consisted of two 'pubs', half a mile apart, with nothing in between! When I asked the roustabout what had happened to the rest of the town, he said, 'This is all they is. One pub to ketch the coves coming from Yass and the other to ketch the coves from Jugiong.'

The track was about half a mile out of the town, unfenced, with no grandstand, and was mostly laid out through a gum and stringy bark scrub. The racehorses were tied to saplings as were hundreds of other horses ridden by wild men from the Murrumbidgee Mountains, who had all brought their dogs. There was a sprinkling of more civilised sportsmen from Yass and Jugiong, black fellows and half-castes from everywhere, and a few out and outers who had ridden down from Lobb's Hole, a place so steep that (as their horse boy said) the horses wore all the hair off their tails sliding down the mountains. The days of racing in heats (i.e. running the horses three times against each other to see which was the best) had died out everywhere except in these outlandish places; but there was one heat race still on the programme. This was the Bogolong Town Flats of a mile, possibly the last heat race that was ever run anywhere.

I had ridden over on a pony with a child's saddle; glancing at the pony to see that he was alright (*sic*), I saw a Murrumbidgee mountaineer about seven feet high taking the saddle off my pony and putting it on a racehorse. Running over to him, I managed to gasp out, 'That's my saddle.'

'Right-oh, son,' he said. 'I won't hurt it. It's just the very thing the doctor ordered. It's ketch weights and this is the lightest saddle here, so I took it before anybody else got it. This is Pardon.' He went on, 'and after he wins this heat you come to me and I'll stand you a bottle of ginger beer.'

In after years a man who speculated largely told me that he could put ten thousand pounds into a speculation without a tremor, but if he put a pound on a horse he could hardly hold his glasses steady enough to watch the race. Imagine, then, the excitement with which I watched Pardon's progress—watched him lying behind the leaders as they went out of sight behind the stringy bark scrub; watched them come into sight again, with Pardon still lying third; and then the crowning moment as he drew away in the straight and won comfortably. Greater still, the delirious joy when he led the field all the way in the second heat, so that there was no need to run a third.

I had the ginger beer—bitter, lukewarm stuff with hops in it—but what did I care? My new friend assured me that Pardon could not have won without my saddle. It had made all the difference. Years afterwards I worked the incident into a sort of ballad called 'Pardon, the son of Reprieve'.

We had eight miles to go to get home, so we had to leave before things got really lively; but before we departed two men had an argument about a bed and each made a run to pull a stirrup iron out of his saddle.

My old friend the sergeant of police from Yass had no objection to a fight, but he drew the line at stirrup irons! He and a mounted trooper handcuffed first one man and then the other with their arms around saplings, a performance which I had never seen before and have never seen since.

As we rode home through the shades of evening, we passed by the door of Dacey's selection; and old blind Geoffrey, a giant of an English agricultural labourer, who was living out his last few years as a pensioner on the bounty of Dacey, came out when he heard the horses.

'Who beat?' he asked.

Of course I had to pipe up that Pardon won the Town Plate with my saddle on him.

'Ar care naught about that,' he said. 'Who beat, the Prodestans or the Carthlics?'

... When I was sent to school in Sydney a new world
opened before me. As a start my cousin and I bought
an old boat, mostly held together by tar, and by way of
brightening up the colour scheme, we painted the floor
with white paint over the tar. This was not entirely
satisfactory, as the tar turned the paint to a sort of un-
wholesome muddy colour, which refused to dry; so then
we had to buy caustic soda to remove both tar and paint
and begin all over again. When we got her finished she
was a fine fishing boat, for there was generally as much
water inside as out, which kept our fish fresh till we got
them home.

But fishing was only a sideline; our real interest lay in
the scullers who worked on the championship course right
in front of our door. Beginning with Hickey and Rush, on
down through Ned Trickett and Elias Laycock, to Beach
and Hanlan, Stanbury and Maclean, last and greatest of
them all, Harry Searle—we knew every man of them,
and could tell them by their styles at three-quarters of a
mile distance.

Stalking with their trainers through the little town of
Gladesville, they were like Kingsley's Gladiators stalking
through the degenerate Romans. Elias Laycock could
eat a dozen eggs for breakfast; Maclean, an axeman from
the northern rivers, could take an axe in either hand,
and fell any tree without stopping for rest; Searle had an
extra rib on either side of his body, or so his opponents
implicitly believed. A flaxen-haired giant, he was the hero
of a queer incident at a dance given at the Gladesville
Mental Hospital. These dances were for the amusement
of the patients, and all visitors were expected to dance
with them. A lady from Sydney, no less than a daughter
of Sir William Windeyer, Judge of the Supreme Court,
was very good natured about it all, and after trotting
several of the patrons out, she invited Searle to have a
turn.

On coming back to her chaperone she said: 'What a pity

that fine young man is mad. He talked quite sensibly until all of a sudden he said that he was the champion sculler of the world. I got away from him as soon as I could!'

These great scullers were mostly young countrymen reared on home grown food, and it would be hard to find their equals in these days of flats and tinned vegetables. The discovery of Beach, the Dapto blacksmith, was due to Doctor Fortescue, a great surgeon of those days, who had his home on the Parramatta River.

Somebody brought Beach to see him, and the Doctor said that he had never seen such a perfect physical specimen. 'This man,' he said, 'will beat that little Canadian' (Hanlan), helping Beach to get boats and a trainer. Hanlan was so superior to all other scullers that the cognoscenti on the river declared that he must have a secret machine in his boat to help him along. This idea was about as sensible as the theory that the Germans, during the great war, had a wireless transmitting station up a gum tree in the Blue Mountains; but people would believe anything in those days and, for that matter, so they will now.

I went to the Sydney Grammar School where I succeeded in dividing the junior Knox prize with a boy who is now a Judge of the High Court. If I had paid as much attention to my lessons as to fish and rabbits, I, too, might have been a Judge of the High Court. There is a lot of luck in these things!

Leaving school, I had a try for a bursary at the University, but missed it by about a mile and half, so I had to go into a lawyer's office. Here I began to learn more of the world. We did a lot of shipping business and one of my first jobs was to go out and gather evidence for the defence of a captain who was prosecuted for not showing a riding-light over the stern while at anchor. Evidence! It was too easy. The captain had seen the boatswain put out the riding-light. The boatswain remembered that riding-light well, as he had nearly fallen overboard while fixing it. The chief officer had been strolling about the deck and had noticed the reflection of the riding-light on the water. I chuckled to think how small the opposition would feel when we unloosed our battery of testimony.

Then the sea-lawyer who was on the Bench, without whys or wherefores, and without summing-up, found the captain guilty and fined him a fiver!

I walked away from the court with the captain and was just starting to speak a piece about the awful iniquity when he said: 'Oh well, I didn't know you had to have a riding-light. They'd drive a man mad with their regulations in these places.' An unnerving experience, but it taught me that a case at law is like a battle: if you listen to the accounts of the two sides you can never believe that they are talking about the same fight.

Later on, I became managing clerk for a big legal firm which did the work for three banks in the depression which preceded the dreary days when the banks themselves had to shut. For months I did nothing but try to screw money out of people who had not got it. Then I went into practice for myself, and of course, was confronted by closed banks. I saw bank booms, land booms, silver booms, Northern Territory booms, and they all had one thing in common—they always burst. My partner and I had banked some money for a client in the Bank of New Zealand and we were told that 'she was sure to shut'. We shifted the money into another bank and the New Zealand concern weathered the storm while the bank into which we had put the money folded up like a blanket!

We managed to keep going even through the depression, and when a cavalry officer came out from England and started a polo club we took to the game like ducks to water. This polo business brought us in touch with some of the upper circles—a great change after the little bush school, the gamecocks, and the days when I looked upon the sergeant of police as the greatest man in the world.

We played a match against the Cooma team, real wild men with cabbage tree hats, and skin tight pants, their hats held on by a strap under their noses. I must have had the gift of prophecy because, before we went up, I wrote a jingle called 'The Geebung Polo Club', a jingle which has outlasted much better work. But this reminds me that it is time to say something about writing.

Up to the time of my arrival in Sydney, all my experiences of life had been limited to contacts with the unsophisticated children of nature. Had I learnt anything from them? Have I learnt anything worth while in the sixty years or so which I have lived since? I take leave to doubt it. There was a time when they called these people the 'great unwashed', but I think that the 'great unsatisfied' would be a better name. Fully ninety percent of people have neither as much money nor as high a social position as they would like, or (as they think) deserve. In those hard times nobody was satisfied, so I thought—like Hamlet—that it was up to me to set the world right. I read heavily in history and economics, and the outcome was my first literary effort— a pamphlet called 'Australia for the Australians'. I blush every time that I think of it.

When my pamphlet fell as flat as the great inland desert, I tried my hand at 'poetry', and strung together four flamboyant verses about the expedition against the Mahdi, who was going well and strong at the time. As the *Bulletin* was the most unsatisfied paper in Australia, I sent them to that paper. I had adopted the pen-name of 'The Banjo', after a so-called racehorse which we had on the station. I was afraid to use my own name lest the editor, identifying me with the author of the pamphlet, would dump my contribution, unread, into the waste paper basket.

My verses actually appeared, and in the same issue was a request that I would call on the editor. Off I went, and climbed a grimy flight of stairs at 24 Pitt Street, until I stood before a door marked 'Mr. Archibald, Editor'.

On the door was pinned a spirited drawing of a gentleman lying quite loose on the strand with a dagger through him; and on the drawing was written: 'Archie, this is what will happen to you if you don't use my drawing about the policeman!' It cheered me up a lot. Evidently this was a free and easy place.

Anyone who wants to know what Archibald looked like should see his portrait by Florence Rodway in the Sydney Art Gallery. It is a marvellous likeness of the bearded and bespectacled Archibald, peering at a world which was all wrong. Not that he ever put forward any concrete scheme for setting it right; he diagnosed the diseases and left others to find the cure.

In an interview of ten minutes he said he would like me to try some more verse. Did I know anything about the bush?

I told him that I had been reared there.

'All right,' he said, 'have a go at the bush. Have a go at anything that strikes you. Don't write anything like other people if you can help it. Let's see what you can do.'

... Other [*Bulletin*] celebrities of the day were Hopkins and Phil May. Except that they were both self taught artists, they were as unlike as possible in every way. A large expansive person named Traill had taken a chance on going abroad and hiring Hopkins in America and Phil May in England. Hopkins was of the large somnolent type; but give him an idea for a comic picture and he would make three jokes grow where only one grew before. May was a bundle of nerves and vitality, wearing himself out before his time. He had learnt his drawings by practising on costers and street-arabs in London.

Hopkins had been reared on a farm in Ohio, and had then, in the American way, taken a job as conductor on a sleeping car so that he might see the world. He practised on the passengers and one has a vision of Hopkins peering round the corridor and working by fits and starts. I think it was Andrew Carnegie who said that, with a bag of oatmeal and determination, a man could teach himself anything. I took Hopkins on a trip—I suppose he would have called it a buggy-ride—down through the rough country to the head of the Murrumbidgee River. He compared everything unfavourably with Ohio until, down on the river flats, I showed him a crop of maize which reduced him to civility. He had to get out of the buggy and handle the maize before he would believe that it was real. Also he said that there was nothing to draw in this unspeakable stringy bark wilderness until we passed an old deserted wool-shed built of slabs and bark, with a big beam sticking out through the top as a lever to press the bales. He said that this in itself was worth the trip, and he spent an hour drawing it and made an etching which I wish I had now. Some day, somebody will begin collecting old Australian work—and those little etchings by Hopkins will come into their own.

. . . Sir Henry Parkes, with his mane of silvery hair and his Nestorian beard, adopted the role of 'the aloof potentate'; in the Argot of the prize ring, he let the other fellow do the leading, and then countered him heavily.

It is said that a field-marshal in war cannot afford to have any friends, and Parkes was a field-marshal plus. Not but what he could relax on occasion but always in an aloof, Jupiterish sort of way. I remember seeing him at a public dinner when the waiter poured him out a glass of champagne from a full bottle and then moved off with it.

'Leave that bottle,' said the statesman, who always got the temperance vote. 'I'll finish that and probably another one after it.'

The old man never had any money, though goodness knows he had opportunities enough of getting it 'on the side' had he been so minded. On various occasions he came into the lawyer's office where I was employed, always full of dignity, in a frock coat and a tall hat, to discuss his pecuniary complications. But personal finance bored him. He despised money; he was Sir Henry Parkes.

Sir John Robertson was also silver-haired and Nestorian-bearded but he was by nature what the Americans call a 'mixer', prone to sit for hours in pubs or clubs entertaining his cronies; in fact, anybody could be his crony, who was found linguistically worthy. He, too, had a rough ride over the financial rocks.

In the gloomy days just before the banks shut I was told by one of them to write Sir John what the bank called 'a nice firm letter', requesting the payment of some money. The old man came in, ran his eye over the office, and asked, through his nose:

'Who's looking after the affairs of the English, Scottish, Continental, Japanese, Australian . . . Bank?'

I said I was.

'Well, you tell them not to write me any more d——d silly letters,' and with that he went off to the club.

The bank asked what reply Sir John had made to the nice firm letter and I said that he had given a nice firm answer.

. . . My bush upbringing had made me tolerant of the battlers of this world, for, but for the grace of God, I might have been one myself. Here is a story of a celebrity with whose career I managed to get mixed up.

In my mail one morning I found a letter from an uncle of mine, a hard-headed grazier who had been through the mill; who had been broke and had made a fortune;

and who had accumulated a great knowledge of the ways of the world.

He wrote: 'There is a man going down from here to Sydney, and he says he is going to call on you. His name is Morant. He says he is the son of an English Admiral, and he has good manners and education. He can do anything better than most people; can write verses; break in horses; trap dingoes; yard scrub cattle; dance, run, fight, drink and borrow money; anything except work. I don't know what is the matter with the chap. He seems to be brimming over with flashness, for he will do any dare-devil thing so long as there is a crowd to watch him. He jumped a horse over a stiff three rail fence one dark night by the light of two matches which he had placed on the posts!'

That same afternoon a bronzed, clean shaven man of about thirty, well set up, with the quick walk of a man used to getting on young horses, clear, confident eyes, radiating health and vitality, walked into the office and introduced himself as Mr. Morant.

'I've been stopping with your uncle, Arthur Barton,' he said, 'and when he heard I was coming to Sydney he told me to be sure and call on you. Fine man, isn't he? He knows me well. He said if anybody could show me round Sydney you could.'

This set things going, so to speak, and the talk drifted from stag hunting on Exmoor to galloping up alongside wild cattle and ripping them with a knife, in the scrubs at the back of Dubbo, which, in those days, was quite far out country. We had a hunt club in Sydney in those days, and he said that he must get a horse and come out with us. He talked like a man without a care in the world. I found myself comparing him with the picturesque heroes of the past who fought for their own hand. Nowadays we would call him a case for a psychologist. Yet, he was no micawber; he did not wait for something to turn up; he tried to turn it up for himself.

Time passed on golden wings while we were chatting
about the bush, and it was just on three o'clock when
he hurriedly looked at his watch. 'By jove,' he said, 'I've
enjoyed myself so much talking to you that I forgot I had
to cash a cheque. And now the banks will be shut. Perhaps
you could cash a cheque for me for a fiver. I've got to pay
some bills and I've run myself clean out of money.'

Almost unwillingly I said that I did not have it about
me, and suggested that he should let his creditors wait
till the banks opened in the morning. He dismissed the
matter with a wave of his hand, and neither then nor at
any other time did he bear any malice for the refusal.

His reputation as a daring rider, and his relationship
to an Admiral, made him a social lion. Asked to stay
with some of our best people he turned up riding a pony,
with his luggage on the saddle in front of him. This
was a great act, and went over big. He got them to take
in the pony for him and borrowed some clothes from
the son of the house who happened to be about his own
size. Then a charity gymkhana was organised, and a
buckjumper was wanted to give tone to the proceedings.
Who could provide a buckjumper so well as Mr Morant?
He fairly lived on buckjumpers away back in his own
wilds. He borrowed ten pounds from the gymkhana
committee to pay the expenses of the buckjumper, a
celebrated grey animal which he meant to bring down
from Dubbo by rail. This also went over big, and people
flocked to the gymkhana to see the celebrated Morant's
celebrated buckjumper. Unfortunately, the man who
owned the buckjumper knew Morant quite well; and while
he was unwilling to lend his animal to anybody, his
unwillingness to lend it to Morant amounted to an ob-
session. Did this disconcert our hero? Not a bit of it. He
went out to the saleyards and agreed with a dealer who
bought horses by the carload to break in for him a grey
horse, one of truckload; and this horse (as it turned out)
knew no more about buckjumping than it knew about

the Einstein theory. The animal's performance at the gymkhana was such a 'flop' that the committee squealed like anything about their ten pounds, and said that they were going to stick to the grey horse until they got their money back. A fair enough proposition, until the owner of the so-called buckjumper turned up and offered to give the secretary of the gymkhana a lift under the ear if he did not give the animal back.

After this our hero's reception at his temporary home was anything but enthusiastic, but, with his queer flair for theatricalism he managed to make an exit with a certain amount of glory. He said that he was called away suddenly to Queensland to inspect a station and as they had treated him so well he wished to present the son of the house with the pony which would be of no further use to him. He would take no denial and he handed over the pony with a sort of Arab's farewell to his steed—a touching scene which lingered in their memories till the owner of the pony cast up and took it away, saying that he had paid Morant a couple of pounds to quieten it for a little girl!

Such was the man who was shot by the British Army after a court-martial for defying army orders and shooting a prisoner in revenge for the death of one of his best friends. I happened to know all that was to be known about Morant's trial and execution, for the lawyer who defended him, one J.F. Thomas, of Tenterfield, asked me to publish all the papers—evidence, cablegrams, decision, appeal, etc.—a bulky bundle which he carried about with him, grieving over the matter till it seriously affected his mind. He blamed himself, in a measure, for the death of Morant, but I could not see that he had failed to do the best he could with a very unpleasant business.

... This was the story of the Morant affair told me by Thomas, and confirmed by reference to his bundle of papers:

'Morant,' he said, 'was detached from his own command in South Africa, and was acting under the orders of a civilian official named Taylor, who knew the country and had been appointed by the army to go round the outlying farms requisitioning cattle. They knew that Morant was a good hand with cattle, so that was how he was put on the job. He had a few men under him and pretty well a free hand in anything he did. They had to keep their eyes open, for wandering bands of the enemy used sometimes to have a shot at them, and in one of these skirmishes a mate of Morant was killed.'

'Morant told me,' said Thomas, 'that he had orders not to let all and sundry wander about the country without proper permit. He questioned a man who was driving across country in a Cape cart on some business or other. According to Morant, he thought that this man was acting as a spy. It so happened that Morant had just seen the body of his mate, and claimed that it had been disfigured; that somebody had trodden on the face. Of course, everybody was excited, not knowing when there might be another skirmish. Morant told his men that he had orders to shoot anybody in reprisal for a murder or for disfiguring the dead or for spying. So he took this man out of his Cape cart and shot him! Unfortunately, the victim turned out to be a Dutch Padre.'

Somehow I seem to see the whole thing—the little group of anxious faced men, the half comprehending Dutchman standing by, and Morant drunk with his own day of power. For years he had shifted and battled and contrived; had been always the underdog; and now he was up in the stirrups. It went to his head like wine.

'Morant was sentenced to death,' Thomas said, 'but I never believed the execution would be carried out. When I found that the thing was serious I pulled every string I could; got permission to wire to Australia, and asked for the case to be reopened so that I might put in a proper defence. It was of no use. Morant had to go. He died game. But I wake up in the night now, feeling that Morant must have believed that he had some authority for what he did and that I ought to have been able to convince the court of it.'

(While he was not unsympathetic, by being so frank about Breaker Morant Paterson had offended against what had become Australian patriotic dogma—that the villainous British had murdered an innocent, cheery chap. The facts of the case were, in fact, worse than Paterson recalled. Morant was involved not only in the murder of one suspected spy, whose Kaffir servant was also murdered, but also in the killing of twelve Boer prisoners on three separate occasions. Still the force of the mythology was such that the Sydney Morning Herald felt that it had to print a footnote from F.M. Cutlack, deploring Paterson's article; he was also attacked in the letter columns.)

In all parts of the world the 'hill billies' are—well, I won't say greater thieves—but they are more enterprising and resourceful than those of the flat. They have to be in order to get a living . . .

The American hill billies who went without boots and lived mostly on plug tobacco and moonshine liquor were classic example. We had nothing quite like them in Australia, but we did the best we could.

By way of curing some sort of nervous breakdown I found myself for some years a hill billy, on 40 000 acres, consisting mainly of country that had been left over after the rest of the world was made.

The place had a history. It had been taken up in the early days by a man who had no capital and no station plant except a wheelbarrow. He built himself some sort of a humpy, got an assigned servant, and set out to build some yards. Yards and a branding iron were all that they wanted in those days to get a start in life. Moving the timber for the yards was a problem, but he solved it by hitching himself on with a sort of harness to the front

of the wheelbarrow, while the assigned servant held up
the handles and 'drove' his boss, giving him such direc-
tions as 'come over to the left a bit,' 'keep away from that
gully,' 'look out the barrow don't run over you down this
slope,' and so on. After a time this got on his nerves and
he sold out to a member of the Ryrie family, who did some
real pioneering. There were girls in the family and one
of them—afterwards known to hundreds and hundreds
of patients as Matron Ryrie of The Terraces Hospital
—killed sheep when the men were not at home, and
carried all the water for the house in buckets from the
river. Then came John MacDonald as next owner, a hardy
and determined Scot, who afterwards became a big
financial magnate and breeder of three Derby winners
at his Mungle Bundle stud; but when he was at this
mountain place he had little else than a branding iron
and a fixed determination to use it. The country was
unfenced, and one could ride for miles and miles in the
ranges seeing nothing but wild horses, wild cattle, wom-
bats, and wallaroos, and hearing at night the chatter of
the flying squirrels playing among the gum tree blos-
soms. His country bounded on a block taken up by a
gentlemen named Castles of Cavan, at one time a school-
master, who had 'gone bush' in the hope of making some
money. Some of Mr. Castles' old pupils, sons of William
Lee, who founded a then priceless stud of shorthorns,
gave Charles some breeding stock—Lee bulls and cows.
A schoolmaster was hardly the man to handle that coun-
try. Some of his young bulls got away, and their stock
ran wild, unknown, unbranded, and mixed up with all
sorts of pike-horned scrubbers which had escaped from
other people.

All those unbranded clean-skins were the lawful prop-
erty of anyone who could yard them; and MacDonald got
them out of the mountains, not in tens and twenties, but
in hundreds. Starting out at daylight with a couple of

cattle dogs and a stockwhip, he took after the wild mobs; and when in after years I asked the oldest inhabitant whether MacDonald had been a good rider, he said: 'Well, nothing out of the ordinary in the buckjumping line, but put him after a clean-skin and he'd show you some class. He'd take two or three falls rather than let a clean-skin get away from him.'

He built trap yards away up in the mountains, sometimes working on by moonlight after his men had gone to camp, and his trap yards were still there when I took the place. Unfortunately, by that time, the supply of clean-skins was exhausted.

It was to this mountain station that I succeeded when I went back to the bush.

As a station proposition it was best avoided; as a homestead there was nothing better. We had eight miles of a trout river, which ran all the year round, clear and cold in summer, a fierce snow-fed torrent in winter. As the sun was setting, the lyre birds came out of their fastnesses and called to each other across the valley, imitating everything that they had ever heard. Gorgeous lories came and sat in rows on the spouting that ran round the verandah, protesting shrilly when their tails were pulled by the children. Bower birds with an uncanny scent for fruit would come hurrying up from the end of the garden when the housewife started to peel apples, and would sit on the window sill of the kitchen, looking expectantly into the room.

Part of the run was enclosed by a dingo-proof fence of thirteen wires, with a strand of barbed wire at the top and bottom; and outside of this there were about ten thousand acres of unfenced country, where one could put sheep when there was any water and chance the dingoes coming in from Lobb's Hole.

One winter they came in when there were a couple of inches of snow on the ground, and the fiery cross was sent round to the neighbouring stations; for the presence of a 'dorg' will make the hill people leave all other work and go after him. We mustered some eight or ten armed men, and as I rode in front on a cream coloured mountain pony I happened to look round at the overcoated and armed figures following me through the snow.

'Where,' I thought, 'had I seen that picture before!' And then I remembered it. Napoleon's retreat from Moscow! I, too, retreated from the mountain Moscow, fortunately with less loss than Napoleon, and resumed city life, not without regrets.

Index of first lines